A Poet Hidden

J. Russell & Sons

Richard Watson Dixon

A Poet Hidden

The Life of RICHARD WATSON DIXON 1833–1900

by

JAMES SAMBROOK

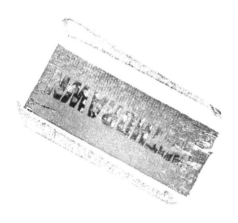

UNIVERSITY OF LONDON

THE ATHLONE PRESS

1962

Published by

THE ATHLONE PRESS

UNIVERSITY OF LONDON

at 2 Gower Street, London WC1

Distributed by Constable & Co. Ltd

12 *Orange Street, London* WC2

Canada

University of Toronto Press

U.S.A.

Oxford University Press Inc

New York

Made and printed in Great Britain by

WILLIAM CLOWES AND SONS, LIMITED

LONDON AND BECCLES

PREFACE

'You will have to be rediscovered after your death like Blake. Some officious Gosse will hang his hat on your tomb', wrote Robert Bridges in a letter to his friend Richard Watson Dixon. As the 'rediscoverer' and the writer of far and away the longest biographical and critical study of Dixon I would seem to lay myself open to the charge of officiousness. However, I hope that my readers will agree that this book is neither superfluous nor disproportionate to its subject, and that Dixon is a poet unjustly neglected. The writer whose verse was admired by contemporaries as discerning and various as D. G. Rossetti, Swinburne, Hopkins and Bridges inevitably claims a passing glance from any student of Victorian poetry, but Dixon is worth attention not only on account of his literary connexions. Professor C. C. Abbott declared that it 'would be no extravagant claim to make for *Mano*' that it is 'the finest narrative poem of its age', and I agree. In Dixon's odes 'On Advancing Age', 'The Spirit Wooed' and 'The Fall of the Leaf', in the sonnets 'To Peace' and 'To Hope', and in 'Fallen Rain', 'Inscience' and some other lyrics in the same narrow range is surely to be found 'the single talent well employ'd'. The *History of the Church of England* holds an established position as a work of scholarship. The appeal of Dixon's writings will probably always be limited, but his fine nature as a man, revealed in Bridges' *Memoir* and in the published letters to Hopkins, cannot fail to attract every reader of those works. I believe that Dixon has some readers today who wish to know more about him and that he ought to have more readers. Therefore I have written my account of his life and writings.

Bridges' affectionate *Memoir* will always be the first source of our knowledge of Dixon the man, standing, relative to its smaller subject, in something like the position of Walton's *Life of Donne*. My book adds much new biographical detail from printed sources and from about three hundred unpublished letters written in the various circles of friends associated with Dixon, and attempts to deal with Dixon's writings much more fully. It supplements Professor Abbott's admirable edition of *The Correspondence of G. M. Hopkins and R. W. Dixon*, which I quote from sparingly since it is easily accessible, and which should be read in conjunction with my Chapters 4 and 5. As I refer to Bridges' and Abbott's books frequently I use the following contractions in footnotes:

Selected Poems for *Poems by the late Rev. Dr. Richard Watson Dixon*, a Selection with portrait and a Memoir by Robert Bridges, 1909.

Correspondence for *The Correspondence of Gerard Manley Hopkins and Richard Watson Dixon*, Edited with notes and an Introduction by Claude Colleer Abbott, 1955.

Although I have been fortunate enough to find an appreciable amount of unpublished manuscript material relating to Dixon (notably the correspondence between Bridges and Dixon which Lord Bridges has most generously allowed me to use), I have had as little success as Professor Abbott had in the 1930s in searches for Dixon's unpublished poems and the diary referred to by Henry Gee in his Preface to volume V of Dixon's *History of the Church of England*. Neither have I been able to find any of Dixon's paintings, or his thirteen letters to the Rev. William Jackson which were described in a catalogue of Myers and Co., New Bond St., in 1936. These are disappointments, but they are, for me at least, offset by the kind welcome and the courteous assistance which has always been given to me in my search for materials. My gratitude is only inadequately shown in the following acknowledgments.

For the use of unpublished manuscript material: Miss Marjorie Barnard, Miss Ruth Daniel, Miss Ethel Hatch, the late Lady Newbolt, Lord Bridges, Mr. Simon Nowell-Smith, Mr. Nicholas Ross, the late Colonel C. H. Wilkinson, the Bodleian Library, the British Museum, Routledge and

Kegan Paul Ltd., the William Morris Gallery at Walthamstow, Worcester College Library.

For permission to reprint published material: Edward Arnold Ltd. for *Letters of G. B. Hill* edited by Lucy Crump, Capt. Francis Newbolt, C.M.G., and Faber and Faber Ltd. for *My World as in my Time* by Sir Henry Newbolt; Longmans, Green and Co. Ltd. for *The Life of William Morris* by J. W. Mackail; Macmillan and Co. Ltd. for *Memorials of Burne-Jones* by Lady Burne-Jones; Oxford University Press for *Selected Poems of R. W. Dixon* edited by Robert Bridges, and *Letters of G. M. Hopkins to R. Bridges, Correspondence of G. M. Hopkins and R. W. Dixon* and *Further Letters of G. M. Hopkins,* all edited by C. C. Abbott.

For help of various kinds: Professor V. de S. Pinto, who was my Supervisor at the University of Nottingham where I wrote the doctoral thesis on which this book is based, and Professor Geoffrey Tillotson, both of whom were kind enough to read my book in manuscript and make extremely valuable suggestions for improvements; Miss Marjorie Barnard, who has allowed me to reproduce the hitherto unpublished photograph of Richard Watson Dixon now in her possession; Bishop J. H. Dickinson, Mr. Simon Nowell-Smith, the Rev. Collin Symes who generously lent me his notes on Dixon and so lightened my early work, Mr. Gwyn Neale and Mr. D. J. L. Moore; and finally, for their never-failing help and encouragement, my parents, to whom I dedicate this book.

J.S.

CONTENTS

1

Youth

Richard Watson Dixon, the eldest son of James Dixon, a celebrated Methodist minister, was born on 5 May 1833 at Islington. His father was then forty-four years old and approaching the zenith of his power as one of his Church's greatest preachers—an orator of magnificent physical presence whose sermons were distinguished by the range of their ideas and the grandeur and vigour of their delivery. Richard's mother, who was James Dixon's third wife and much younger than her husband, was the daughter of another great Wesleyan leader, Richard Watson. She was a sensitive, nervous, excitable and learned lady. The child, commemorating in his names the most famous Methodists of the age, spent his early boyhood within the limited circle of his own family and the society centred upon local Methodist chapels. As several daughters had been born of James Dixon's earlier marriages and five more brothers and sisters eventually joined Richard, the boy grew up within a large and self-sufficient family, self-sufficient not only because of its size but because of its inability to take root in any one place, since the Methodist Church demanded that its ministers should stay no longer than three years together on one circuit.

Richard's wanderings began when he was a year old, for in 1834 his father was appointed to a Liverpool circuit, where he remained for the customary period of three years.

In the third year of his ministry the accession of Queen Victoria brought a General Election with all its attendant violence, which Mrs. Dixon described in a letter to her husband who was away at the annual Methodist Conference:

We have gained a glorious triumph, but I fear at the cost of many lives. Lord Sandon had a majority of 502, Cresswell 372! Is it not wonderful? The town has been a horrible scene of riot and bloodshed. The whole Irish population has been up, and awful the confusion. The soldiery have been called in from Preston, and somewhere else, and the Riot Act read. In our quiet spot I have been greatly excited, and ventured out as far as the market, but was glad to take refuge in a druggist's shop, to escape a mob of the most infuriated, hellish wretches, belabouring one another with great clubs. I ran home as fast as I could, and have kept all within doors. A large crowd of Sandonites came down our street with drums and colours, so I made little R[ichard] hold out of the window a piece of scarlet ribbon and shout 'Sandon for ever!' which he did most manfully; and they stopped and gave us three hearty cheers. I was determined that his first shout should be for Toryism.[1]

The incident impressed young Richard and he remained a lifelong Tory.

To some men the violence of the 1837 election seemed to herald revolution, and in the 1830s and 40s, when workmen who massed at Radical meetings wore tricolour cockades and caps of liberty, often it appeared that the 'living Chaos of Ignorance and Hunger' was about to rise in protest against poverty and squalor. Much of Richard's childhood was spent in the industrial north, close to the sources of this revolutionary agitation, for his father's ministries took the family to Sheffield, where they lived from 1837 to 1840, to Manchester, 1840 to 1843, and later to Birmingham. In the West Riding in 1839 the Chartists were armed and planning a widespread insurrection, there were strikes and rioting in Manchester in 1842, and always during these years there was some unrest in the north. In his childhood Dixon saw not only the violence of revolt but its causes, and his

[1] R. W. Dixon, *Life of James Dixon, D.D.*, 1874, p. 202.

knowledge of the hideously insanitary industrial towns with their miserable inhabitants shaped his later views on social problems. But the immediate effect upon him of living in these surroundings was that he suffered ill health. Public Health improvements had scarcely begun; disease easily and often came out of the slums to invade middle-class homes, and there was frequent serious illness in the Dixon family. An infant daughter died during the years at Liverpool, in Manchester the health of most of the children was bad, and it became worse when the Dixons moved to London in 1843 and lived for a short time in Poplar.

It was here that Richard, ten years old and desperately ill, conceived a liking for *Paradise Lost*. His love of the poem waned as he recovered his health and a taste for more mundane things, and his father felt compelled to admonish him in a somewhat predicatory letter:

I thought perhaps you had lost some relish for this sublime and glorious poem, now that you are in better health, and can associate more with the world. I hope, if it should be so, you will return to the region of poetry and religion, as the most pure and ennobling. What are all external things compared with the spiritual, the holy, the invisible, the eternal? You had a strong impression of the supremacy and glory of such things, I am persuaded, at the time in question, and such feelings and impressions should never be lost. To converse with God, with the heavenly world, with all the divine and mighty influences and agencies which are abroad in the universe, with the angelical and spiritual world, with Jesus Christ, His apostles, martyrs, confessors, and followers; with the great truths and designs of the Gospel and kingdom of God—to think on these things, and fill the mind with noble sentiments and feelings from these great fountains of truth and purity, is much more elevating than anything else can be. Keep to Milton, and the spirit and grandeur of poetry.[1]

However, the father's fears of worldliness in his son were needless. Much of Dixon's boyhood reading was in devotional works (he read with delight Bishop Hall's *Contempla-*

---

[1] *Life of James Dixon*, pp. 283–4.

tions and Law's *Serious Call*), and in health as in sickness he
shared the spirituality of his parents. Daily prayer and the
reading aloud of devotional literature, as practised in
middle-class homes, were not to all as unwelcome and
meaningless as they were to Samuel Butler. To many people,
including the Dixons, family prayers were pleasing and
beneficial, and when James Dixon declared 'No sight on
earth is so lovely as that of a pious family living in the
constant habit of family prayer and praise, and thus rendered harmonious by the pious and affectionate union of
every member',[1] he described his own family. This family, in
its turn, saw him as a man living upon 'a vast height of
holiness'[2] and, although lovable and admirable, difficult to
approach because of his melancholy and stormful nature.
His impact upon the life of his Church was considerable, for
his ministries were successful and famous and he rose to
become President of the Conference in 1841; in national
affairs he made his mark too, as spokesman for Methodism
in the Maynooth controversy of the 1840s; and his influence
was correspondingly great within his own family. Richard
wrote:

> It was an ennobling influence; but there was always an awe
> and a reserve which no tenderness and intimacy ever overcame.
> . . . There was melancholy, reserve, and silence, and strong
> individuality impressing itself involuntarily upon all around: but
> beneath this such tenderness and affection as are inconceivable
> and inexpressible. The majesty of his character impressed and
> indeed awed all who were in immediate contact with him; but at
> the same time the deepest affection was mingled with the venera-
> tion produced.[3]

Perhaps the weighty presence of a father of such distinction
and strength of character was partly the cause of Richard's
lifelong diffidence and impressibility. As a child he was
timid, solitary and reserved, and although in manhood he
inherited his father's spiritual greatness he lacked his
father's power and command.

---

[1] *Life of James Dixon*, p. 145.   [2] *Id.*, p. 476.   [3] *Id.*, pp. 276, 280, 281.

Richard was stamped for life with many of his father's opinions on religious, political and social questions, but did not follow him into the Methodist Church, for, at the age of fourteen, he was confirmed in the Church of England. This, however, was no great departure from Methodism, since conservative Wesleyans, such as James Dixon, were more friendly towards evangelical Anglicanism than towards the great body of Dissent. In the year of the confirmation, 1847, the Dixons spent some time at Richmond. Richard was admitted to lectures at the Methodist College there and sat near the lecturer answering correctly questions that had defeated the class. Such precocity was the result of a home education at the hands of gifted parents and long hours in his father's library of historical and devotional works. The stay at Richmond was a delightful interlude in a life spent largely in drab cities. There James Dixon and his slim, stooping, dark-haired, serious and diffident son were able to take long walks together in earnest conversation, shortly afterwards recalled by the father in a letter:

I thought of our conversation about the Duke of York—Nelson—War—Genius—and felt distressed at the idea that I should never take the same walk with you again. I have been to-day along the other path, that is, along the terrace, Lord John Russell's, through the gate into Ham Common, down the road where we looked at two beautiful cottages with roses and flowers in full bloom in front, and offered some useless wishes for such an abode for ourselves; then past the good tailor's where you bought the buttons, and so on up the road below the Star and Garter, and found my way home for dinner. . . . It is now growing dusk, and I have finished, most likely for ever, my connection with this beautiful place. The walks have ended and these associations are broken up. I shall see you no more at this lovely spot—and I, and you too, must hasten to plunge into new and untried scenes. May God prepare and be with us.[1]

The untried scene into which the Dixons plunged in September 1847 was the young borough of Birmingham, a busy, sprawling, squalid town where Chartism had recruited

[1] *Life of James Dixon*, pp. 282–3.

much of its power and where the vigour of the Radicals allied with Nonconformist conscience and organizing ability had only recently begun to make social conditions better. Although its prosperity was growing its population had multiplied much too rapidly, and the town had been allowed to develop into a vast warren of mean streets and undrained, ill-ventilated, filthy courts, often visited by typhus. Richard and his contemporaries found a Birmingham that 'reeked with oil and smoke and sweat and drunkenness', and they might well have agreed with the French visitor who said that the town seemed to be 'a thousand leagues from the civilized world'.

The Dixons came to live in Hockley on the northern outskirts near to the famous Soho Works, and on 5 October Richard was admitted to King Edward's School, which at that time occupied Barry's new but gloomy 'resuscitated Tudor' building in New Street. The school was beginning to enjoy a considerable reputation for scholarship and religion, for its headmaster, James Prince Lee, was a 'maker of men' who maintained a tone of stern piety in his school and drilled Christianity into his pupils somewhat after the manner of Dr. Arnold, under whom he had taught at Rugby. He had been a distinguished classical scholar at Cambridge, and beneath his headship the Birmingham school produced in the 1840s three of its most brilliant men, Westcott, Lightfoot and Benson. However, Lee found Dixon far less brilliant than these, for, owing to his delicate health and his parents' migratory way of life, the boy had never been to school before. His wide reading in English devotional literature, that had seemed so impressive at Richmond a few weeks earlier, could not save him at Birmingham.

At that time he knew nothing whatever of arithmetic, could only make great botches for writing, and knew not a word of Latin or Greek. He had read, however, more English books than almost any boy in the whole School. He was put in the lowest class among the little boys, and the first thing they gave him to learn was the 'Propria quae maribus' without a translation, or any explanation as to its meaning. He did his best, and at the

6

end of an hour was called up to say six lines or so, but could not say a word. For this he was caned, and told to bring up ten lines the next morning. He took the book home, worked at it all the evening, learning while undressing and dressing and on his way back to school; but when called up could not do any better than before. For this he was taken to Prince Lee, who caned him and publicly degraded him to the bottom of the school, and there he stuck for some time, being flogged every day, till he did not care any more about it. One day he had written his exercise with rather more blots than usual, and the writing-master told him to show it to the Headmaster. Dixon marched up with a perfectly cheerful air, caring nothing about the punishment expected, and said with a happy tone, 'Mr. — has told me to show you my copy book.' [Lee], judging from his tone that he must have done well, opened the book, and turning back to the previous exercises, happened to light on one even more blotted. 'Well,' said he, 'I am glad to see there is *some* improvement at last', and sent Dixon back to his place in triumph. The writing master, noticing his pleased air, asked him what the Headmaster had told him. Dixon answered that he had said 'he was glad to see there was *some* improvement'. At this the master charged him with having prevaricated, but never sent him to [Lee] again.[1]

The two hundred boys in the Classical Department of the school were taught in one room. 'The Babel was awful', says an old pupil,

but it taught us to shout and was probably good for the lungs. The din was increased by the outside street traffic. . . . Only boys of exceptional ambition or wits could make decent progress. A boy never dreamt of asking explanations of his difficulties: the free use of the cane alone could drive us forward until we reached the higher classes.[2]

By the beginning of 1850 Dixon had been flogged up to the second class and was studying in a comparatively rarefied atmosphere at the less crowded end of the classroom.

In his short story *The Rivals* Dixon wrote

I am constitutionally very delicate; was sent to school late, and passed all my schooldays in my native place, one of the

---

[1] L. Crump (ed), *Letters of George Birkbeck Hill*, 1906, p. 54.
[2] G. Burne-Jones, *Memorials of Edward Burne-Jones*, 1904, i. 15.

largest manufacturing towns in England. . . . Among my school-fellows I was liked, being considered, though very shy, yet anxious to please. . . . [My speculation] upon others implied, of course, a continual comparison of others with myself; and, being joined with a natural timidity, or, as I have called it, impressibility, whilst it gave me considerable insight into character, rendered me, above all things, desirous to adapt myself to the different people into whose society I was thrown. Thus was formed in me, almost from the beginning, a dangerous habit of self-introspection, and a nervous wish to give pleasure at any cost.[1]

Dixon himself was just as impressible as the first-person hero of his story, and so the companions of his schooldays left their mark upon him. After an early boyhood that had been lonely, sheltered, and strongly dominated by his father, Dixon gained at school the invigorating friendship of one man of genius and several of exceptional talent who gave him an important intellectual stimulus and helped him to shape his views on many matters. The shy, melancholy and solitary boy felt the scope of his life widened as the frank friendships of youth freed him to some extent from acute self-consciousness and timidity.

In his first years at school he had no special companions, although he met some men slightly older than himself—William Fulford, R. J. Whitehouse and Wilfred Heeley—who were later to become his close friends. It was not until autumn 1850, when he was joined in the second class by Edward Burne-Jones, that his circle of firm friends began to form. Like Dixon, Jones was nervous, sensitive and pious, and suffered from delicate health and melancholy. Both were imaginative, loved history and literature, and shared a desire to read 'all that there was to read'. Soon Dixon came to know Jones's closest friend Cormell or 'Crom' Price, a little later he became friendly with Price's form-mate Harry Macdonald, and the circle was completed about the beginning of 1852 with the inclusion of Edwin Hatch.[2]

[1] *Oxford and Cambridge Magazine*, 1856, pp. 34–5.

[2] Price became headmaster of the United Services College at Westward Ho! and is represented as 'the Prooshian Bates' in *Stalky and Co.* Mac-

Dixon was able to make and maintain school friendships only because his stay in Birmingham was unusually long, for when James Dixon's three years on the West Birmingham circuit came to an end in 1850 he was appointed to the East circuit. The family thereupon moved to the opposite side of the town, to live on the Coventry road, and Richard remained at King Edward's School. He was living less completely within the family now that he had found at school companions more sympathetic than his brothers and sisters (who did not share his own interests), and perhaps he was finding his family in some respects oppressive. There is a story that Dixon once arranged to go to a theatre with Jones and that Dixon's mother, regarding theatre-going as evil, was so worried as to urge that if her son went she should go also. However, in the event, 'she walked with her boy to the place of meeting, in order to see what the tempter was like, and after looking at him left the two together'.[1] Dixon himself throws some light on his home life when he says of Jones, 'I remember envying his position [i.e. in his own home] as he was evidently lord, and did as he liked, asking whom he would to visit him: which was out of the question with me. He always used to have money and nice things about him, to schoolboy extent.'[2]

In the lower forms of the school Dixon had displayed an early facility in authorship. He was once found in class causing much noise and laughter among his neighbours by reading a story to them, and when his manuscript was confiscated by a teacher it proved to be a highly sensational Tale of Terror, after the manner of *The Mysteries of Udolpho*, in which a German baron threw his wife and daughter from a castle rampart into the moat. Dixon was writing verse too, and in the higher forms of the school he won more than

---

donald went to America and became a journalist. He was the son of a Wesleyan minister and brother of the four ladies who became Lady Burne-Jones, Lady Poynter, Mrs. Alfred Baldwin (mother of the first Earl Baldwin) and Mrs. J. L. Kipling (mother of Rudyard): see A. W. Baldwin, *The Macdonald Sisters*, 1960. Hatch became a famous theologian: see *D.N.B.*

[1] *Memorials of Burne-Jones*, i. 53.   [2] *Id.*, i. 50.

once the annual prize for English verse. He was acknowledged as the poet among his circle of friends, so that when
Heeley tells Fulford what honours their friends ought to
enjoy in later life he reserves the Poet Laureateship for
Dixon.

By autumn 1851 Dixon, Jones and Macdonald had moved
up into the first class and were more directly under the
supervision of the headmaster Edward Hamilton Gifford,
who had succeeded Lee. Dixon's older friends had now gone
up to university. In the more adult atmosphere of the first
class the boys discussed the greater problems of the day:

> A considerable section of the upper boys were quite awake to
> the crying evils of the period; social reform was a common topic
> of conversation. We were nearly all day-boys, and could not
> make short cuts to school without passing through slums of
> shocking squalor and misery, and often coming across incredible
> scenes of debauchery and brutality.[1]

The school had a religious tone[2] and so the pupils became
absorbed in religious controversies also. Dixon's friends
represented widely different doctrinal viewpoints and
argued among themselves continually, especially over the
Gorham Case. Jones, as leader of the schoolboy High
Church party, was eager to win over Dixon to his side; so,
after their voluntary attendance at Gifford's Sunday afternoon Greek Testament classes, the two boys would walk up
and down New Street for many hours arguing the knotty
question of Baptismal Regeneration.

A month after the Gorham judgment the death of Wordsworth provoked another kind of nation-wide debate. But
over the Laureateship Dixon and all his friends were united
and were Tennysonians to a man. Their enthusiasm for this
poet, before he became the bard of Victorian society and

---

[1] J. W. Mackail, *Life of William Morris* (New Edition) 1901, i. 64.

[2] Which on the side of the staff was characterized by a gloomy insistence
upon the penal aspects of religion, if we may generalize from the pamphlet
addressed to Dixon's contemporaries by C. P. Male, an assistant master at
the School—*Have you any fear of death? A Word of Advice to the Young;*
suggested by the recent death of a pupil of King Edward's School, Birmingham, 1851.

the revered oracle of his age, was wild and uncritical; Tennyson was their literary idol and Fulford was his high priest. Before meeting Fulford, Dixon had always regarded Cowper, the Methodists' favourite, as the greatest English poet. However, he read Tennyson's *Poems* in the school library, was at first puzzled, and then, after Fulford's exegesis, admired them. When *In Memoriam* came into the library it was read with reverent delight by all the friends and thereafter, up to the publication of *Idylls of the King*, Tennyson could do no wrong. *Maud* was the last poem that mattered, for its hero voiced that dissatisfaction with the times and those vague yearnings for a fuller spiritual life that Dixon and his friends felt. But it was Tennyson's magical powers of incantation which swept them away at first:

> The fascination of such lines as
> > 'Listening the lordly music flowing through
> > The illimitable years'
> when first heard, was indescribable. So of all of The Dying Swan, The Lady of Shallott. . . . I think the line
> > 'I heard the steeds to battle going'
> in Oriana, equal in what one may call epic painting to any line of Virgil or Milton,

wrote Dixon.[1] He and his friend Heeley were provoked by Tennyson's verse into a new way of looking at things and writing about them—'a sort of transcendental feeling, which we called meteorosophia'.[2] Dixon, in his turn, infected the others with his own love of Keats, who was not very widely read in the 1840s. The group's literary tastes were exclusively romantic; they loved *Christabel*, the traditional ballads, Scott and Byron.

Dixon's friends were touched by that tide of revolutionary feeling which swept across Europe after 1848, and they cheered the triumphal progress of Kossuth through the streets of Birmingham on 10 November 1851. They rebelled against their seniors' complacency, so strikingly evinced in

[1] Letter to Robert Bridges, 16 November 1892.
[2] Letter from Dixon to Bridges, 21 January 1893.

the Crystal Palace in the same year. Their discussions on
religion, art and politics had convinced them that their
world must be regenerated, so they drew together into what
Gifford was to call the 'little band of Knights of the Round
Table who were to go forth from School and conquer the
world'.[1] But the idea of such a brotherhood had hardly been
distinctly formulated when Dixon left school in summer
1852 to go up to university.

The last important event in his school life was the Ter-
centenary Celebration on 16 April 1852, when there were
processions and speeches, the pupils were feasted with cakes
and wine, and Dixon was awarded a prize for his essay on
'The State of Literature in England in the time of Edward
VI.' This year he won, not for the first time, the prize for
English verse. His prize poem, 262 lines long, is a narrative
in decasyllabic couplets of the Sicilian Vespers massacre. It
was printed and a copy has survived.[2]

The Sicilian Vespers is a competent prize poem which reflects Dixon's boyhood reading in Keats. The following
passage adequately displays the poem's literary ancestry,
and demonstrates a love of rich colour that brings Dixon
close in spirit to the Pre-Raphaelite painters:

> The smothering sunshine of Sicilia's noon
> Was melted into eve: the day-long swoon
> Of nature was fulfill'd, while twilight brings
> Her shade-engrained coolness, from her wings
> Shaking the dew bells; and the golden haze
> Of sunset was upon the daedal maze
> Of nature,—deepening the orange gleams,
> Glossing smooth olive leaves, empurpling streams,
> Gilding brown tree-stocks, glowing through the grapes,
> And dancing on the corn-tops; till the shapes
> Of the whole valley fruitage seemed a mass
> Tangled of light and shade: above there was,
> In th'upper air, one vast unbroken rain

[1] Letter to Rev. W. Rees, in Bodley MS.,Don.e.20, fol. 51.
[2] *The Sicilian Vespers, a Prize Poem*, by R. W. Dixon, King Edward's
School, Birmingham, Midsummer 1852. The only copy I have been able to
trace is in the City of Birmingham Reference Library.

Of tremulous lustre; for the sunbeam train
Fell not on earth, save where some distant peak
Brow-bound with rosy snow, stood up to break
That soften'd glory streaming forth so wide,
Like to a river isle, round which the tide
Disparts: and evening's breathing gently stirred
The locks of Flora; that light sigh uprear'd
On Ocean's face no frown-ridge; he lay spread
All waveless, windless, on his sandy bed.

This is comparable with the richer and rosier sunset in
Hopkins's 'A vision of the Mermaids', also the work of a
Keats-intoxicated youth.

2

The Brotherhood

Dixon matriculated at Pembroke College, Oxford on 3 June 1852 and came into residence in the following October. Soon he renewed his ties with two older King Edward's School men at the College, Whitehouse and Fulford, and they introduced him to another Pembroke man, Charles Joseph Faulkner.[1] A Birmingham friend, Wilfred Heeley, was at Cambridge, but maintained a voluminous correspondence with Fulford. After Whitehouse had been ploughed in Divinity in Moderations and had gone down, Fulford was left to preside over the 'Set' that grew up during the next two years. But although at Oxford he was the leader of a group of highly gifted men, some of whom were later very distinguished, his undergraduate superiority did not foreshadow any lasting achievements of his own, and he faded into obscurity soon after leaving Oxford. He was ordained, published four volumes of verse, and remained a curate for most of his life.

Dixon had come up without an exhibition or other award and the allowance of £100 a year given by his father barely covered his needs. Birkbeck Hill says he was unpopular with a section of the Pembroke undergraduates because he could not contribute to the College Boat Fund, but that during the Crimean War when a subscription was raised for the

[1] A mathematician, later Fellow and Tutor of University College, Oxford, and partner in Morris, Marshall, Faulkner and Co.

Florence Nightingale Fund he gave more than anyone in the College. His few attempts to blossom forth as a 'swell' were perhaps regarded less seriously by himself than by Hill, who records their failure: 'If he had a new suit of clothes and a new hat, his shoes were sure to be as much worn as were Johnson's when they provoked the scorn of the Christchurch men. If his shoes were new, his hat was old.'[1] But his comparative poverty did not trouble him unduly, and he came to Oxford full of eagerness and high hopes.

In 1852 Oxford was still small and old. Seen from a distance, its towers appeared to rise up directly out of a space of meadows and orchards. Much of its common street architecture was of the fifteen century, and amongst the colleges the depredations of Butterfield, Waterhouse and Scott had scarcely begun. Oxford gave Dixon and the friends who sooned joined him there an ideal physical setting for their plans to reform the world through a 'restoration' of the Age of Chivalry, but she gave them nothing else—or so they thought. They brought intellectual vitality, high ideals and corporate enthusiasms bred from their schoolboy discussions, and they found only indifference. In later life Dixon once called the University a 'cruel stepmother' and of Pembroke he wrote

> I am not willing to say much, but I did not find it in a good state. The Master did nothing in tuition except a Sunday Lecture in Greek Testament. There was very little discipline, no social intercourse between the fellows and the undergraduates, and Collections were merely a nominal ceremony.[2]

Edwin Hatch was more outspoken:

> I shall be very glad to migrate from Pembroke. I really can't find anything to admire in it, and I am sure that it is a delusion to imagine that it is less expensive than any other place. I neither like the lectures, nor, (with few exceptions) the men, nor (I regret to add) the chapels, for we reverse the order of things and gallop through the service with a volubility which leaves

---

[1] *Letters of George Birkbeck Hill*, p. 50.
[2] Douglas Macleane, *A History of Pembroke College, Oxford*, 1897, p. 460, n.

our thoughts far behind our words, and it only takes fifteen minutes or less for full evening prayers. As for lectures . . . I have long since ceased to hope that I shall learn anything at them which I did not know before. . . . Imagine yourself ushered into a large room comfortably provided with chairs and a large centre table. The men take their places round it, and the lecturer, looking up from his easy chair by the fire-side exclaims: 'Will you go on Mr. —?' The approved crib version is then faithfully given, and meanwhile most other men are getting by heart or otherwise Bohn's translation of the next piece. When No. 1 has concluded, the lecturer asks benignly '*Dum* governs two moods, doesn't it?' 'Yes.' 'It governs the subjunctive some-times, doesn't it?' 'Yes.' 'Is *qui* ever used with the subjunctive: it is, isn't it?' 'Yes.' 'Very well, *very well*, Mr. —. Will you go on Mr. —?' 'Haven't read it?' 'Oh never mind then, you go on Mr. —, will you?' And when the crib has been deposited in the hands of a neighbour in order that any requisite emendations may be whispered into the man's ear, the lecture proceeds. At some awful blunder, up jumps the lecturer, and after a long yawning pause, mildly breaks forth. 'Well yer know, I should *hardly* think you'ld take it in that way, yer know. Mr. — will you just translate that passage?' (Another crib version is given.) '*Precisely* so, precisely so, quite right, *quite right* Mr. —.' And so we gradually limp through a page or two, which none of the men have bestowed ten minutes upon, and leave the room for another exhibition of crib repetition. I am giving you a very faint notion of the reality, but as one evidence that it is bad enough. I would mention that I have not yet heard one single thing worth putting down in a note book.[1]

This was the scene presented to the serious and pious Dixon when he came up to Oxford with a headful of romantic literature and vague aspirations to do great and good things for the world. However, in the Michaelmas Term of 1852 Dixon and his friends had not yet planned their crusade against what they saw as an ugly, rationalist, materialist and over-complacent age. They did not begin to do this until after Jones had come up to Exeter College in January 1853 and had brought into the group his new friend William Morris.

[1] MS. 'Life of Edwin Hatch by his Widow', p. 33.

Jones's letters picture vividly these early days of the Set, and afford us brief glimpses of Dixon:

[Fulford] slangs and I growl, and Faulkner demonstrates, and Dixon translates himself into the seventh heaven of poetry. . . .

Dixon is another fine fellow, a most interesting man, as ladies would say—dark-haired and pale-faced, with a beautiful brow and a deep melancholy voice. He is a poet also. I should be sorry to dash the romance of his character, but truth compels me to say he is an inveterate smoker.[1]

A slightly fuller account of Dixon is provided by a younger contemporary, Birkbeck Hill:

I still recall the wonder with which I watched Dixon as he sat in an arm-chair by the fire smoking a long 'church-warden'. His complexion was unusually dark, and his hair was black. 'Black Dixon' was the name he went by among those who did not know him. From time to time he would join in the conversation in a deep, slow voice, in striking contrast with Morris's quick eager tones. I looked upon him as an oracle of wisdom. He was always known as 'Dickadees', as Morris was 'Topsy' or 'Top', and Jones was 'Ned'. . . . To very few men indeed was he known, but those who knew him well loved him for his great simplicity of character. He was 'an Israelite indeed in whom was no guile.'[2]

On May Day 1853 Jones wrote to Price

10 o'clock, evening. I have just been amusing myself by pouring basons of water on the crowd below from Dixon's garret, such fun, by Jove. . . . I have set my heart on our founding a Brotherhood. Learn Sir Galahad by heart. He is to be the patron of our Order.[3]

It is clear from other letters by Jones during this year that he wished to organize among his Oxford friends a celibate society to do social work in the poorer parts of London. Such projects were popular in the aftermath of the Oxford Movement and would appeal to the piety and social

[1] *Memorials of Burne-Jones*, i. 74, 123.
[2] *Letters of George Birkbeck Hill*, pp. 49, 50.
[3] *Memorials of Burne-Jones*, i. 77.

conscience of the Set. Fulford, Dixon, Jones and Morris all intended to enter the Anglican ministry and there can be no doubt that their schemes for a brotherhood to carry out social reform and moral self-improvement were bound up with their religion, but I wonder whether this conventual design of Jones arose from a true sense of monastic vocation or was just one of those Pantisocratic schemes devised in youth by many groups of close friends who wish to translate their friendship into a permanent institution. They had determined to conduct a 'Crusade and Holy Warfare against the age' but had no definite programme of action. They were, as one of them said,

disturbed by a vague yearning after they scarcely know what, unsettled by discontent with the things which lie around them—to use language as vague as their desire, longing after some more spiritual life, which, however alien it might appear to their ordinary habits, they yet feel, indistinctly enough it may be, to be in harmony with their true nature.[1]

They were never able to state their objects finally because their outlook was always widening. Every new interest they acquired and every new book they read could be the germ of a new crusade.

Carlyle, Charles Kingsley and Ruskin were prominent among the prophets who first inspired them. Dixon approved of the writings of Kingsley and Carlyle on social reform but, significantly, preferred Charlotte Yonge's more genteel advocacy of philanthropy in *The Heir of Redclyffe*. Miss Yonge was a votaress of Keble and Dixon admired the High Anglican spirit of her book. He regarded the pious, refined and chivalrous Sir Guy Morville, with his daily acts of self-discipline and his eagerness for social reforms (effected from above), as a model for his own life. Over forty years after coming down from Oxford he said it was 'unquestionably one of the finest books in the world'; and in their younger days none of the friends would have disputed

---

[1] W. Fulford, 'Alexander Smith' in *The Oxford and Cambridge Magazine*, 1856, p. 550.

this judgment. *The Heir of Redclyffe* led them to Lamotte Fouqué's *Sintram and his Companions*. In this Christian allegory with gothick décor they found valuable moral instruction, but the tale appealed also by its weirdness. Traces of *Sintram* may be found in Jones's drawings of 'horribles and things', in the drear landscapes of Morris's early tales and in some of Dixon's more occult poems.

Fouqué's book was linked with that 'grey, shadowy, many-pinnacled image of the Gothic spirit' which was always present in the minds of the friends, shaping their schemes for social reform and colouring their religion. Among their gospels, beside *Past and Present* and *Sintram*, they placed the chapter 'Of the Nature of Gothic' in *The Stones of Venice*. Dixon, Jones, and Morris all responded to Ruskin's call for Christian art and thereupon found that the real bond between them was artistic rather than religious. Dixon wrote, referring to their intention of taking Orders,

> We never spoke of it to one another: and I am sorry to say, for my own part, that it was not contemplated, or kept before the mind. The bond was poetry and indefinite artistic and literary aspirations: but not of a selfish character, or rather not of a selfseeking character. We all had the notion of doing great things for men: in our own way, however: according to our own will and bent.[1]

In their changing projects there was a slow shift from religion to art which was completed near the end of their Oxford days when, through Ruskin, they came to know Dante Gabriel Rossetti and accepted his leadership.

In autumn 1853 the Dixons moved from Birmingham to Liverpool when James Dixon was reappointed to his old circuit there. In October Fulford, Faulkner, Dixon, Jones and Morris were together again in Oxford, drinking tea by firelight in Faulkner's room, punning, ragging one another and settling 'once for all how all people should think'. 'We chatted about life, such as we knew it, and about ghosts, which Dixon believed in religiously but Faulkner despised,

---

[1] Dixon's MS. notes for Mackail (in the Morris Gallery, Walthamstow).

and many an evening we wound up with a bear-fight', recalled Jones.[1]

In summer 1854 Morris drank the delights of Gothic
architecture to the full in Belgium and northern France;
Jones got as far afield as Sydenham where he was unim-
pressed by the Crystal Palace ('give me', he said, 'The
Light of the World and the apse of Westminster'); while
Dixon spent the long vacation at home in Liverpool. At the
end of the vacation Jones was still scheming for his monastery. He wrote to Price

> You were surprised no doubt at the postponement of term. It
> made me very angry, for I was sick of home and idleness and
> longed with an ardent longing to be back with Morris and his
> glorious little company of martyrs—the monastery stands a
> fairer chance than ever of being founded; I know that it will be
> some day.[2]

When term did begin, a week late on account of the terrible
cholera epidemic of that autumn, Price came up to Brase-
nose to complete the ranks of the noble army, or, as they
now called it, the Brotherhood. Hatch, at Pembroke, and
Macdonald, at Corpus Christi, had come up earlier that year.
The life of the Brotherhood continued in a ferment of
debates and plans, with long afternoon expeditions out into
the countryside, meetings of the University Plain Song
Society of which Dixon, Jones, Morris and Price were members, weekly Shakesperian readings, and always the long
talks in the evenings on painting and architecture and
literature and metaphysics and the regeneration of society.
At the end of the year Morris suddenly disclosed that he was
a poet. Dixon was astonished by the beauty and power of
his *The Willow and the Red Cliff*; 'Well', said Morris, 'if this
is poetry it is very easy to write.'

During 1855 the hopes and aims of the leading members
of the Brotherhood became increasingly secularized. In the
previous year Ruskin's *Edinburgh Lectures* had introduced

[1] *Memorials of Burne-Jones*, i. 106, 107.
[2] Mackail, *Life of Morris*, i. 63, 64.

them to Rossetti's name, Jones and Morris had seen pictures by Hunt and Rossetti and had read *The Blessed Damozel*, and they had fallen under Rossetti's spell. Fulford had gone down but was hesitating to enter the Church. Dixon was thinking less of ordination than of his literary aspirations. In May Price declared 'Our monastery will come to nought.' At Encaenia Tennyson took his D.C.L. degree. Dixon was present at the scene of wild enthusiasm that greeted the Nation's Greatest Poet, Fulford came up for the occasion and the friends enjoyed themselves boating, promenading and breakfasting. Fulford and Jones went off with Morris in the long vacation to study the art and architecture of northern France, and on the return journey Morris and Jones made their resolution not to take Holy Orders but to hurry their Oxford lives to a close and become architect and painter. Dixon and Fulford, after hesitation, chose the Church, and, although they continued to write verse, were unable to live as wholly for their art as Jones and Morris had resolved to.

For some years the Brothers had lived largely to themselves, nourished by their own dreams in the seclusion of their colleges, but in the summer of 1855 they decided to come before the world and see what practical reformation their missionary zeal could effect. They took up eagerly Dixon's suggestion that they should start a magazine containing poems, tales, 'friendly critiques' and social articles which would advocate moral earnestness in literature, art and society. This would be no ephemeral University journal but a national periodical conducting a crusade against the materialist assumptions of Victorian society. Discussion on the magazine continued throughout the long vacation. On 6 October Price received letters from Morris and Dixon, 'both sick of aimless, theoretical lives', and a week later the Brotherhood, including Fulford who had come up to coach Morris for his pass degree, was reunited.

Dixon was now living out of College, and the friends used his small front parlour in Pembroke Street as a regular meeting place, where they listened to his dissertations upon

Intellectual Transcendentalism and his exposition of what were, for Hatch at least, 'exploded theories' in theology. There, too, the lighter-minded members of the group were once amazed by his refutation of Sir David Brewster's *More Worlds than One, the Creed of the Philosopher and the Hope of the Christian.*

> If there are other worlds inhabited by man, he said, there must in each have been the temptation and fall of man, to be followed in each case by the sufferings of the Saviour. 'This is too horrible to contemplate', he added in a low tone.[1]

It was in the Pembroke Street rooms that the Brothers planned their magazine, read over their literary efforts and praised one another's powers. As the publication date of the first issue drew near their fighting spirit rose, and Jones wrote

> We have such a deal to tell people, such a deal of scolding to administer, so many fights to wage and opposition to encounter that our spirits are quite rising with the emergency. . . . We may do a world of good, for we start from new principles and those of the strongest kind, and are as full of enthusiasm as the first crusaders, and we may perish in a year as others have done before. Well, if we are wanted I suppose we shall remain, and if not, what have we to want? Nothing, I know, for I can safely affirm for all that no mean and contemptible desire for a little contemporary fame, no mere purpose of writing for writing's sake has prompted one amongst us, but a sole and only wish to teach others principles and truths which they may not know and which have made us happy.[2]

The first monthly number of *The Oxford and Cambridge Magazine, conducted by members of the two Universities* appeared on 1 January 1856. The contributors were Heeley from Cambridge, Morris and Jones (two pieces each), and Fulford, Dixon and Macdonald (one piece each), but the only work of any permanent literary value is Morris's poem *Winter Weather.* Dixon's tale 'The Rivals' does not deserve

---

[1] *Letters of George Birkbeck Hill*, p. 50.
[2] *Memorials of Burne-Jones*, i, 121, 123, 124.

much of our attention. It displays its author's reverence for the work of Miss Yonge and Tennyson and his proclivity towards morbid self-analysis, its portrayal of unhappy adolescent love shows some insight but is hardly extraordinary, while the plotting of the sentimental story is feeble. Other prose contributions included Fulford's inevitable eulogy of Tennyson, the story of an imaginary medieval church by Morris and an essay by Jones on *The Newcomes* which is remarkable chiefly for a digression on book illustration that praises *The Germ* and Rossetti's illustrations to *Day and Night Songs*.

Of this last essay Rossetti wrote to Allingham

> That notice in *The Oxford and Cambridge Mag.* was the most gratifying thing by far that ever happened to me—being unmistakeably genuine . . . it turns out to be by a certain youthful Jones . . . whom . . . I have now met. One of the nicest young fellows in—*Dreamland*. For there most of the writers in that miraculous piece of literature seem to be. Surely this cometh in some wise of the *Germ*.[1]

The meeting between Jones and Rossetti had taken place in the Christmas vacation, when Jones had seen Rossetti over a mug of tea in F. D. Maurice's Working Men's College and a few days later had visited him in his studio. The consequence of the meeting was that, after a few half-hearted attempts during the Lent Term to read for his degree, Jones left Oxford and placed himself as a pupil under Rossetti. Morris had already gone down, although he remained in Oxford studying architecture; Dixon and the younger Oxford men were working for Schools and Faulkner was trying for a fellowship. So during the year after the launching of the *Magazine* its projectors became increasingly possessed by other interests. It was owing partly to this and partly to decreasing circulation that the *Magazine* ceased publication after twelve monthly numbers.

The February and March issues contained two articles by Dixon on the Crimean War—'The Barrier Kingdoms' and

[1] G. B. Hill (ed.), *Letters of Dante Gabriel Rossetti to William Allingham 1854–70*, 1897, pp. 173, 174.

'The Prospects of Peace'—which are the *Magazine*'s only excursions into international politics. Like most of his contemporaries Dixon thought that after the fall of Sevastopol the Allies were in a winning position and ought not to come to an early peace that might leave Russia still strong and dangerous. 'The Prospects of Peace' is the latest contribution that can be attributed to Dixon. Strangely, no verse by him was published in the *Magazine*.

In the second half of 1856 most of the Brothers were losing interest. In September Fulford wrote 'Topsy and I are the only ones of the set that write at all regularly' (they had written three pieces each of the eight which made up that month's issue). At the end of the long vacation Heeley was married and shortly afterwards went out to India. The wedding brought together nearly all the Set, but Dixon was not there. He was moving home from Liverpool to Manchester with his father's now diminished family, for his mother and one of his sisters had died in April. On 7 September he wrote to Price about Morris's recent visit to the Low Countries, 'Topsy has written me a long account of the peregrination. The same little brick has sent me the Seven Lamps.' Before the end of the year Morris was living in London with Jones and had been induced by Rossetti to give up architecture and become a painter. On their week-end visits to the Oxford Set Jones and Morris carried back Rossetti's doctrine that all men should paint (except those who should buy pictures), and the Brothers set to work to paint or draw or model. The union between Rossetti, Jones and Morris was now very close, and Rossetti was sufficiently interested in the *Magazine* to contribute to it three of his finest poems. He deeply regretted its extinction, which came after a year's steady decline in sales, accompanied by a decline in its projectors' enthusiasm for it. The December issue was the last. It demonstrates admirably what was worst and what was best in the *Magazine* by bringing together the fifth long instalment of an encomium upon Carlyle by Vernon Lushington, a Cambridge Brother, and Rossetti's 'The Staff and the Scrip'.

The Oxford and Cambridge Magazine is remembered today only on account of the tales and poems of Morris and Rossetti. But their work is untypical of the *Magazine* and differs as greatly in kind as in quality from the contributions of the others, most of whom take their lead from Fulford, sometimes repeating his ideas and often capturing his magisterial dullness. The heat of Fulford's enthusiasm had done much to weld together the Brotherhood at the beginning, and it was thanks largely to his energy that the *Magazine* remained alive as long as it did, but his dominating literary influence was not beneficial. Little of Fulford's personal vivacity and attractiveness found its way into his literary style. His poems are Tennyson-and-water or Wardour Street balladry and his essays pompous, while the turgid style of his tales achieves a kind of 'Spasmodic' prose which wearies the reader. Most of the tales by Fulford and his imitators explore situations of undeclared or unrequited love. Their misunderstood, sensitive heroes have stepped from the pages of *The Heir of Redclyffe* or *Maud*, but perhaps also reflect the Brothers as they saw themselves. Nearly all these tales touch upon the 'Condition of England question', and several of the essays take up this theme too. Inevitably their writers frequently invoke the names of Ruskin and Carlyle. These tales and essays of Fulford and his 'school' examined the condition of England and demanded that it should be improved through individual spirituality and a sense of social duty; Morris's work, on a much higher literary plane, reacted to a hateful environment by taking the path of escape into a glamorous idealized world of the imagined past. Thus the *Magazine* showed the two possible responses by sensitive men to the materialism and ugliness of the age. The work of Morris and Rossetti was unnoticed by the readers of 1856 and could not keep the *Magazine* alive, while the *Magazine* did not deserve to live by virtue of the rest of its contents. Owing to financial backing by Morris it lasted longer than its archetype *The Germ* and, unlike *The Germ*, it did not have to resort to burlesque and a partial abandonment of principles in a struggle to remain alive. Resolutely adhering to its first aims it made no concessions to popular taste; it contrived to be earnestly and consistently dull and had no hope of long continued survival.

In December the *Magazine* petered out and Dixon came down from Oxford with an inglorious third class in Greats and no immediate intention of entering the Anglican ministry. Old idealisms had flowed into new, and the 'Knight of the Round Table' who had gone up to Oxford to bring about a restoration of the Age of Chivalry and had stayed to become in turn a prospective monk and a journalist now came down a Pre-Raphaelite artist. When he went home to Manchester for Christmas his father was dismayed to learn that he had decided to become a painter—a decision that had been made after Jones had taken him to see Rossetti, declaring as they went 'We shall see the greatest man in Europe'. Twenty-five years later when Dixon recalled this meeting and described Rossetti he still adopted the attitude of a disciple, emphasizing those characteristics which made Rossetti influence other men:

I saw Rossetti for the first time in his lodgings over Blackfriars Bridge. It was impossible not to be impressed with the freedom and kindness of his manner, not less than by his personal appearance. His frank greeting, bold, but gentle glance, his whole presence, produced a feeling of confidence and pleasure. His voice had great charm, both in tone, and from the peculiar cadences that belonged to it. . . . The main features of his character were, in my apprehension, fearlessness, kindliness, a decision that sometimes made him seem somewhat arbitrary, and condensation or concentration. He was wonderfully self-reliant. These moral qualities, guiding an artistic temperament as exquisite as was ever bestowed on man, made him what he was, the greatest inventor of abstract beauty, both in form and colour, that this age, perhaps that the world has seen. . . . When he chose to be interested in anything that was brought before him, no pains were too great for him to take. His advice was always given warmly and freely, and when he spoke of the works of others it was always in the most generous spirit of praise. It was in fact impossible to have been more free from captiousness, jealousy, envy or any other form of pettiness than this truly noble man.[1]

Rossetti's frankness and generous capacity for friendship endeared him to the open-hearted enthusiasts of the Brotherhood, and it is not surprising that Dixon succumbed to his spell just as the less impressible Jones and Morris had done. At this time Morris and Dixon were primarily poets, but as Rossetti had in his own work subordinated poetry to painting he persuaded them to do likewise. So for some months during 1857 Dixon was given instruction in painting by Rossetti. This tuition may have taken place in the first half of the year, for which period I have found no record of Dixon's whereabouts, or in the later months when Dixon and Rossetti were certainly together in Oxford and London. Two paintings by Dixon have been recorded. Beeching writes in his *D.N.B.* article on Dixon of 'a wedding scene from Chaucer', and Bridges' *Memoir* of Dixon includes a reference to a painting of mountains. I have been able to trace neither of these pictures.

By the middle of 1857 the Set revolved round Rossetti. In July he visited Oxford and declared that the wall above the gallery bookshelves in the newly built Union Debating Room was 'hungry for pictures'. So he proposed a scheme for covering the ten bays of this wall and the ceiling with paintings in tempera of scenes from the *Morte d'Arthur*. The Union agreed to pay for materials and to lodge and feed the workers recruited by Rossetti, but not to pay for the work itself. Eventually six artists, Val Prinsep and Spencer Stanhope (young disciples of G. F. Watts), J. H. Pollen, Arthur Hughes, Jones and Morris, joined Rossetti in what came to be called 'The Jovial Campaign', but when they came to begin work in August all seven were equally ignorant of the peculiar technique of mural painting. They began hastily and ran into innumerable difficulties as they attempted to paint on an unprepared surface of damp mortar and whitewashed, uneven brickwork.

[1] T. Hall Caine, *Recollections of D. G. Rossetti*, 1882, pp. 37–9.

A brief visit by Dixon to France coincided with the beginning of the Union paintings, but before the long vacation was over he was back in Oxford helping Morris to paint those towering sunflowers in the foreground of his Palomides and Tristram scene. The life led together by the seven painters and the remaining members of the Set when they came up was full of horseplay, puns and endless talk as in the heyday of the Brotherhood. 'What fun we had in that Union!' recalled Prinsep,

> What jokes! What roars of laughter. . . . Rossetti was the planet round which we revolved, we copied his very way of speaking. All beautiful women were 'stunners' with us. Wombats were the most delightful of God's creatures. Mediaevalism was our *beau idéal* and we sank our own individuality in the strong personality of our adored Gabriel.[1]

Dixon was happy in his new and old friendships. He was writing occasionally for periodicals and was full of plans, but had no clear notion of what direction his life should take. A letter to Hatch, dated October 1857 from Manchester, bears this out:

> I feel like a hideous criminal, but I *have* written to you—do you hear—I *have* written & you evidently did not get my letter dated to the Poste Restante at Milan. Faulkner said something to me about *his* having also written to you without the shot telling. And now I feel I owe you a long letter in answer to the many you have delighted me with. You jolliest and most mysterious of men! How *do* you manage to lead such a stunning life as you do? Eh? How, oh Epicurus how?
>
> You will be surprised to hear that I too have been on the Continent—to Paris for a week & Amiens for two days. This was after your return, and the opportunity was presented in a very unexpected way. I must have been in London at the same time but knew it not. I am tired of making engagements, but do hope to get off into Europe next year, & may it be with you. I cannot express the bitterness of my disappointment at failing you this year: but it was absolutely unavoidable. My brothers are likely

---

[1] *Memorials of Burne-Jones*, i. 163–4.

to want all the money my Governor & I can get for them in Australia &c.[1] Oh dam.

As to the main proposal in yr. last letter but one, about working at Plato, I can only say at present that I regard it very favourably, that I fully agree with you that Plato has never been understood, that I have great confidence in you, and sd. most desire to work with you since we could afford to give each other the broadest scope for developing our own peculiarities and yet work harmoniously together—I am sure of this with you—and, finally, that it is manifestly suicidal, & insanely unjust to ourselves to be wasting our lives & the freshness of our powers upon periodicals. We cd. live up at the Lakes for £50 per annum apiece, & work undisturbed. I regard the scheme most favourably: but can scarcely yet return a definite answer. Perhaps you will also require to reconsider it. Write when through the schools. By Jove I wish you the best of luck. But it wont very much matter if you mucker. My own mucker is quite a forgotten thing with me. Does not affect me in the least except for good. i.e. it has kept me from grinding in some wretched school.

.... Your loving brother
Dickides

Although Morris had finished his share of the Union decoration in November the work of some of the others dragged on well into the winter. Patmore and Ruskin came and admired, but the painters were bored and the Union was apprehensive about expense. After March of the following year the seven artists did no more and the remaining three bays were filled by William Rivière. The story of the decay of the pictures and their restoration in this century is well known.

For a month or two in the winter 1857–8 Dixon was living in the little Bohemia of Jones and Morris's lodgings at 17 Red Lion Square. But despite the inspiration and tuition of Rossetti he found that he could not continue his career as a painter. His family was not wealthy, so he could not afford to train as an artist and, perhaps with justification, he lacked confidence in his own talent. It may have been partly the force of these considerations that made him take Holy

---

[1] Two of Dixon's younger brothers had emigrated in 1856.

Orders, although his later life confirms that his true vocation was, after all, to the Anglican ministry. The work on
Plato was shelved, the paints were put away, and in the
Easter and Trinity terms of 1858 Dixon was back at college
preparing for ordination.

Both Dixon and Hatch were Oxford prizemen this year.
Hatch won the Ellerton Prize, and Dixon the Arnold
Historical Essay Prize with his 'The Close of the Tenth
Century of the Christian Era'. Dixon's essay is interesting
chiefly because it is an early study of the period in which he
was to set the events described in his most important poem
Mano. The essay reveals his excitement when viewing an
age whose people lived in daily expectation of the end of the
world. Dixon looks at the events and persons of the Tenth
Century against the light of an Apocalyptic vision, and so
his account of them is more strange and powerful than is
usual in an historical work. Although the essay's thesis that
the Tenth Century was greatly obsessed by dread of the
Millennium is historically unsound, as an imaginative picture of cosmic twilight and terror it is quite remarkable.

When Hatch read his Ellerton Prize essay in the Divinity
Schools in June many of the Brothers were there to hear
him. This was one of their last large meetings in Oxford.
Shortly afterwards Dixon was ordained deacon and became
a curate of St. Mary the Less, Lambeth, in the Deanery of
Southwark where junior clergy were notoriously underpaid
and overworked. The parish contained about fifteen thousand people, most of whom belonged to the labouring
classes. There was a great deal of destitution, and the vicar
Robert Gregory, afterwards Dean of St. Paul's, was working
hard bringing relief and employment to his parishioners,
establishing schools and restoring a long-neglected church
building. Dixon threw himself eagerly into parochial duties
and pleased his vicar greatly with his hard work. Inevitably
he saw much less of the Oxford Brothers now.

In April 1859 Morris was married to Jane Burden in
Oxford. Dixon came up from London to conduct the service,
'and, to the satisfaction of his friends who had warned him

against it until he could do nothing else, ended by pronouncing the young couple to be man and wife together under the names of "William and Mary"'.[1] Morris and his wife came to live in London while the 'Red House' was being built at Bexley. Meanwhile Dixon was ordained priest and continued in his parochial round, to the dissatisfaction of Fulford who wrote in a letter—

One hoped that Dixon would make a poet. I at one time felt quite confident of it, and I must say I regard any success in practical life (though the life and duties of a clergyman) as a poor substitute for this, perhaps the highest work allowed to human nature. I may be unfair in applying this to Dixon, for he not only reads but also writes poetry, and that I fancy in considerable quantity, but still I should like to see him living a definitely and manifestly poetical life, such as Edward's, [i.e. Jones], whom one feels to be in the right path, pursuing the course which nature marked out for him.[2]

Certainly Dixon was greatly occupied by his practical life, nevertheless his poetical life was occasionally made manifest; as, for instance, when he was discovered lying flat on the ground in the vestry making verses, and, when asked if it was not an uncomfortable position, replying 'Oh no, I was absorbed in the Infinite.' His youthful ideals and enthusiasms were still unimpaired, and his laudation of Ruskin's *Modern Painters* in the *London Quarterly Review* of October 1860 drew what must have been a gratifying acknowledgment from Ruskin:

there are expressions of praise in this review which proceed only from kind sympathy—and which are far overwrought and unjustifiable—as the writer will in time discover; but the kind patience of analysis is calculated to be of the greatest use to any reader caring to read the books seriously:—in some sort it even helps me myself—for knowing the consistency and constancy of my principles at their roots, I have always allowed myself to work out any consequences, or seize on newly apparent classifications, without looking back—or at least with very casual looking

[1] *Memorials of Burne-Jones*, i. 194.
[2] *Id.*

back—to any that had gone before, and sometimes when I *do* look back, I don't myself see the connection, though I know there is, or was, or some day will be, one.

I have been not a little helped today by reading this review—being at present in a state of considerable vexation with everything I have ever said or done.

Little is known of Dixon's life as a curate, but his days could not have been dull if incidents like this one, recorded by Robert Bridges, were commonplace:

having to offer thanks for the churchwarden who was sitting in his pew again for the first time after a dangerous illness, he proclaimed in a mighty voice that that gentleman desired to give praises to God for his safe deliverance from pain and peril of child-birth. It was Dixon who told me the story, how for the rest of the service he and his victim were the only two persons in the church who maintained a decent gravity; and he imitated, without a smile on his own countenance, the stuttering and spluttering of the Vicar, who could not bring his trembling lips together to pronounce the p's in 'The Epistle is taken from the Epistle of Paul the Apostle.' When the end came, Dixon avoided the congregation by traversing the bye-streets, but a like motive and knowledge of the locality prompted the churchwarden to make a somewhat similar détour, and their courses brought them together alone at a corner face to face.[1]

Bridges adds 'This incident was of the kind that did not assist Dixon's worldly progress.' This may be so, for the next stage of Dixon's worldly progress took him no farther than the curacy of St. Mary's, Newington Butts, to which he was appointed in 1861 and where he stayed for less than a year. While there he was married on 9 April 1861 to Maria Thomson, a widow twelve years older than himself, with three daughters. He assumed all at once a large burden of family responsibility and retreated into obscure domesticity.

---

[1] *Selected Poems*, pp. 188–9.

3

Christ's Company
and
Historical Odes

Preoccupied with his work and his family and no longer under the immediate influence of his early friends, Dixon put aside his youthful undertaking to reform the whole of society. After living in the Brotherhood in a white heat of communal enthusiasms for ten years he sank into that cooler, mundane and 'unpoetical' life which Fulford so deplored, and the last act of his youth was to publish in 1861 a collection of his early verse under the title *Christ's Company and Other Poems*.

Much of the verse in this volume is derivative, some, indeed, is mere *pastiche*, and much of this derivative verse is stamped with the marks of Pre-Raphaelitism, marks, that is, from Rossetti's rather than Hunt's die. In the dramatic monologue 'St. John', the longest of those High Church hagiographical pieces which compose 'Christ's Company', we find that dreamy, decorative medievalism, with heraldry, emblems, elaborate pictorial detail and more than a hint of the 'aesthetic swoon', which characterized the later stages of Pre-Raphaelitism:

> Came in their battles, all the seraphim
>   With giant plumes, with glory-beaming eyes,
>   Long bands and wrapping robes, in solemn guise,

Came Michael, and an army followed him;
  His sword, two-handed, carried he before,
His vast eyes on the hilt, his shield's broad rim
  Swung half of it behind him; in the score
Of his knights followed all the cherubim;
  And half the stars shone in his banner wide
  And in it all the winds were multiplied.

Came Gabriel, with his banner over him,
  White lilies, brass-bright flowers, and leaves of green;
A lily, too, he carried seemed to brim,
  With golden flames, which mounted pure and clean
To touch his blessed mouth, and then would trim
  Themselves within the lily leaf again:
  Gabriel's fair head sank even with dream-pain.

As 'St. John' is an exercise in the Pre-Raphaelite manner, so the other long poem in the 'Christ's Company' group, 'St. Paul, Part of an Epistle from Gallio, the Deputy of Achaia, to his brother Seneca' (referring to the events of *Acts*, xviii, 12–17), is an imitation of Browning. Dixon makes Gallio speak with the faint awareness of Christianity of a Cleon or a Karshish, and throughout his poem he echoes Browning's allusive, broken, conversational style.

'Love's Consolation', which is the longest of the 'Other Poems', owes something to Browning, but seems to echo Morris more. Dixon intended this poem to be a prologue to nine tales about the 'Crosses of Love', but the series was never finished.[1] The narrator of 'Love's Consolation', a

---

[1] Two of the tales, 'Concealment' and 'Perversity', appeared in *Historical Odes*, 1864; but Dixon had difficulty in finding plots suited to his purpose, so that only two more tales had been written by 1880, when he described the scheme to Bridges:

'My original notion was to get stories to illustrate some point in the course of hapless love, as Concealment (done), Perversity (done), Cross Purposes (done), Too much Friendship (done), Rivalry, Mischance (like Romeo and Juliet), Jealousy, Treachery, Absence, Delay, Care.' (*Selected Poems*, pp. xxviii, xxix.)

The tale of 'Cross Purposes' was 'Love's Casuistry', which is now lost; 'Too Much Friendship' was published in *Last Poems*, 1905.

Dixon's list for Bridges ennumerates eleven crosses of love, but it is clear from his letter to Rossetti (see p. 56 below) that his earlier plan was to have nine, one for each lover in the Monk's vision in 'Love's Consolation'.

Monk of Osneyford, who presumably was to have told all
the tales, is an attractive figure of a type used more than
once by Dixon—an old, placid and garrulous scribe who
looks back upon a wild youth. The knights and their ladies
('stunners' all) whom he sees in a vision could have stepped
from a Burne-Jones canvas or the pages of *The Defence of
Guenevere*:

> And then nine gentle forms did I behold—
> Five men and four sweet ladies, as I told—
> All walking towards me, with a gentle pace,
> Round from the thorn, all with full solemn face,
> And head bent solemnly: to me they came,
> One led the band, the rest led each his dame.
> The first who came waved forth a long green wand,
> Whereat the others in fair show did stand
> Divided, four on either side, a knight
> And queen together, on the left and right.
> Those knights had golden crowns upon their heads,
> And their long hair drawn out with golden threads,
> And rightly were they harnessed, and each bore
> A coronal of thorn leaves, with good store
> Of berries red, which shone like drops of wine
> Amongst the green leaves and the gold wire fine.
> Those four queens wore the thorn-leaves; I saw there
> Red berries spread about upon their hair:
> Their crisped tresses hung more clear and fine
> Than yellow amber holding gold-red wine;
> Their looks were wildly gentle, and more fair
> Than full-eyed fawn just shaken from her lair.

Many of the poems in *Christ's Company* have some such
obvious literary affiliation as these three, and Professor
Abbott has shown[1] that they may be grouped into the
'schools' of Tennyson, Browning and Morris. But although
Dixon often speaks with the accents of other poets he
has, in his more serious poems, something of his own
to say. In 'St. John', for instance, the Pre-Raphaelite

[1] *Correspondence*, p. xviii.

devotional word pictures are mounted upon a theological
framework:

>   let me think to keep my soul
> Fixed . . .
>   on the whole
> Of love in love divinely multiplied;
> Not generated in the onward roll
>   Of ages, though to men 'tis centuried;
> But rather in all points of time perfected,
>   As in the bosom of the mind divine,
>   So in the thoughts of life which thence outshine . . .
>
>   for say, was I not found
> In the blest bosom of that love, which slakes
> Our human thirst, when all the rest at gaze
>   With distant eyes were murmuring, Is it I?
>   Lord, is it I? And think ye no reply
>
> Did make me nearer to the hidden ways
>   Of love, no response beat into my ear
> From that deep heart which pulsed the awful rays
>   To the eyes beneath whose curve I did upsteer
>   My reverend gaze, whilst holding solemn state
> In the upper room;—no benediction pressed
> Like a spear's head of bliss into my breast? . . .
>
> The bliss renews itself in visions still,
>   And urges me for ever to aspire
> To that great knowledge which drew out my will
>   To ecstasy, as fire to flame draws fire.

The fact that religious doctrine (especially the central
Christian doctrine of the Incarnation) and experience, albeit
clumsily expressed, occupy so prominent a place in his Pre-
Raphaelite verse distinguishes him from his greater Pre-
Raphaelite colleagues—Rossetti, who uses religious symbols
only as decorations, and the secular Morris and pagan
Swinburne. The three important longer poems, 'St. Paul',
'St. John' and 'Love's Consolation', are not free from
obscurities, but their general drift is clear. They declare a

belief in the happy purposefulness of life and assert that
divine love—'love in love divinely multiplied' ('St. John'),
'love, the infinite in nature spread' ('St. Paul')—'o'er-
spreads in genial current all things' ('Love's Consolation').

Dixon's meaning is less explicit in some of the shorter
poems. In 'Eunice', for example, the reader suspects that
there is a private mystery within the poet's reach but
beyond his, while Dixon again fails to give adequate verbal
expression to his intuitions in 'The Soul's World', where he
attempts to picture the human mind in terms of a strange
landscape. In 'Despair', however, he has more vividly
realized an esoteric vision of the more frightening regions
of the soul's world and the enigmatic shapes that haunt
them:

> I find myself by a black spring and cold,
>   Which slowly bursts from this rock's heavy head,
> Like drops of sweat wrung from our God of old,
>   And plashes dead
> Into a basin hollowed from the mould.
>
> I trace this fountain rolling deeply down—
>   Dark is the night, my pathway ruinous—
> Here foam the muddy billows thick and brown,
>   Then issue thus
> Into a lake where all the world might drown.
>
> I mark the mountains stand about and brood—
>   The lake and they together, God, remain,
> As black and deep and steep as walls of mud
>   On some vast plain
> Block out and brood upon a swimming drain.
>
> I mark a woman on the farther shore
>   Walk ghost-like; her I shriek to with my might;
> Ghostlike she walketh ever more and more;
>   Her face how white!
> How small between us seems the Infinite!

Ghastly landscapes are found too in 'Proserpine', which
paints a picture of subterranean fire and sacrifice as murkily

as befits a poem on the Eleusinian mysteries. There are
more dabblings in the supernatural in the nightmarish
'Dream', and in 'The Wizard's Funeral' where Dixon
blends an element of terror with a filmy snatch of Blessed
Damozellery:

> Yet think of half the world's winged shapes
> Which have come to thee wondering:
> At thee the terrible idiot gapes,
> At thee the running devil japes,
> And angels stoop to thee and sing
> From the soft midnight that enwraps
> Their limbs, so gently, sadly fair;—
> Thou seest the stars shine through their hair,

and ends with a well-judged 'turn of the screw',

> I go to a mansion that shall outlast;
> And the stoled priest who steps before
> Shall turn and welcome me at the door.

The individual vein of weird terror running through 'Despair', 'Dream' and 'The Wizard's Funeral' is discernible
elsewhere in *Christ's Company*—in the ill-organized 'In the
Woods' for example, where it outcrops oddly among
Wordsworthian reflections—but disappears from Dixon's
work after his Pre-Raphaelite phase.

His later verse was to be marked by that less forced
strangeness which is found in these passages from two very
uneven poems: 'The Wanderer',

> Oft by the marsh's quaggy edge
>   I heard the wind-swept rushes fall;
> Where through an overgrowth of sedge
>   Rolled the slow mere funereal:
> I heard the music of the leaves
>   Unto the night wind's fingering,
> I saw the dropping forest eaves
>   Make in the mere their water ring . . .

But day by day about the marge
Of this slow-brooding dreaminess,
The shadow of the past lay large,
And brooded low and lustreless;
Then vanished as I looked on it,
Yet back returned with wider sweep,
And broad upon my soul would sit,
Like a storm-cloud above the deep:

and 'La Faerie',

I sought the wild path of the soaring moon . . .

But when she levelled with the horizon's mound
Her speckled mirror, speeding fast away,
Then every spot and tuft upon the ground,
Rounded with shadow, domed and coned, and gray,
And shaking with the secrets of the wind,
Circled my feet so lovingly, and made
Their signs to me, that I no farther strayed;

Until the lion colour, which had skinned
The nether clouds, had left them black and vast
In the moon's setting; then too paled and thinned
The unshaped purpose which had bound me fast;
And all was withered, dark, and gray again:

and from 'To Shadow',

If ever thou didst creep
From out the world of sleep,
When the sun slips and the moon dips,
If ever thou wast born;
Or upon the starving lips
Of the gray uncoloured morn.

If ever thou didst fly
In the darkness of the sky,
When it was shaded and cloud-invaded,
And thou didst form and flit
By the wild wind aided,
Like a phantom shed from it . . .

> If ever thou didst pass
> Into blue along the grass,
> And into blue the long wood through,
> When the sunset lay within't,
> And thou hast touched anew
> Into softness every tint.

Dixon's landscapes are drenched with the poet's feelings and appear to be haunted by a strange shadowy life. Hesitantly at first, Dixon is beginning to pick out his maturer 'tune'.

There is a great deal of faulty craftsmanship in *Christ's Company*. Dixon makes perverse metrical experiments; in 'St. Paul', for instance, he creates difficulties for himself by adopting the unaccommodating rime scheme—ababcccc-dcdeeee . . . etc., with the four consecutive rimed verses octosyllabic and the other decasyllabic. Often he brusquely overrides his metrical difficulties. But his technique is not always faulty. In the 'Sonnet' there is a varied harmony, a fine economy of suggestion and a perfect suiting of poetic means to ends that make it, at the lowest reckoning, one of the best of the effusions of the huge tribe of minor nineteenth century sonneteers:

> Give me the darkest corner of a cloud,
>   Placed high upon some mountain's lonely head,
> Craggy and harsh with ruin; let me shroud
>   My life in horror, for I wish me dead.
> No gentle lowland known and loved of old,
>   Lure me to life back through the gate of tears;
> But long time drenched with rain and numb with cold,
>   May I forget the solace of the years:
> No trees by streams, no light and warmth of day,
>   No white clouds pausing o'er the happy town;
> But wind and rain, and fogbanks slow and gray,
>   And stony wastes, and uplands scalped and brown;
> No life, but only death in life: a grave
> As cold and bleak as thine, dear soul, I crave.

Moreover Dixon has discovered how to use the decasyllabic couplet for easy, steadily flowing narrative, and, years before the appearance of *The Earthly Paradise*, he shows in his 'Love's Consolation' a mastery of a transparent Morris-like style, developed not by imitation of Morris but by a study of Morris's original, Chaucer:

> It being then the happy Christmas time,
> And all the orchards thick with frosty rime,
> I took me by the happy paths that go
> Along the dumb and frozen river, so
> That I might taste the goodness of the day;
> Passing through many meadows on my way,
> Where all the grass and flowers were dead asleep,
> Through many sheepfolds full of bleating sheep,
> By many watercourses, whereby grew
> The little-headed willows, two and two,
> And also poplars: onward thus I sped,
> Until the pathway reached a little head
> Of brushwood, screening up a wicket gate,
> Whereat I entered, and beheld elate
> A wide and scattered wood of late-leaved beech
> And oaks and thorn-trees, standing on the reach
> Of long-withdrawing glades: at sight of these
> And the snow-dabbled grass, and broken knees
> Of large red ferns in patches, as I went,
> Felt I great exaltation and consent
> Unto the sweetness of the place and day:
> The robin called the merle, who was away,
> And yet the robin answered from his bough:
> The squirrel dropt from branch to branch, although
> Few leaves did screen him; and with frequent bounds
> The rabbits visited each others' mounds,
> And o'er the dead leaves pattered.

When all the incompetent or merely derivative work in *Christ's Company* is sifted out a small body of original and interesting verse remains, comprising 'St. John', 'Love's Consolation', 'Eunice', 'Dream', 'The Wizard's Funeral', 'Despair', 'The Soul's World', 'To Shadow' and parts of other poems. Here we find, variously, Christian hope and joy with occasional hints of a personal mysticism, an individual vein of romantic strangeness, and the first intimations

41

of that delicate sympathetic insight into external nature which later will produce those poems that I regard as peculiarly Dixonian. Lacking judgment, Dixon published with his good poems a great deal of verse that should have been excluded—such juvenilia as 'Babylon and Nineveh' (based on his reading Layard in the King Edward's School Library) and the boyish-Keatsian 'Vision of Thebes', and such an esoteric burlesque of Morris and his Oxford sun-flowers as 'Romance'. The reviews inevitably seized upon the bad work. *Fraser's Magazine* declared 'we doubt whether Johnson's college will be very anxious to claim Mr. Dixon among its literary notabilities',[1] and went on to quote from the worst parts of 'The Wanderer', 'Waiting' and 'Romance'. The *Athenaeum* reviewer read the more import-ant religious poems but seems not to have understood them. He wrote 'His religious feeling is of a morbid and sombre kind; he makes his devotions gloomily, in sackcloth and ashes', and added a little more percipiently 'His poems display thought; but his reflective powers are obscured by diseased imagination and bad taste.'[2] Where *Christ's Com-pany* was not received with hostility it met indifference, and Dixon may have been looking back to its reception when he wrote many years later, referring to episodes in his father's youth,

Youth, if it aspire at all, knows only of the ardour within itself—knows little of its own powers. The ardour is so intense as to fill the whole consciousness, and make all things seem possible. The attempt is made; the untried powers are put forth to the utmost, and, if success does not instantly follow, disap-pointment is felt in all its keenness. If to the want of success be added ridicule, the greatest pain is then endured that can fall to the share of rectitude and high intentions.[3]

At the end of 1861 Dixon left his curacy and went as an assistant master to Highgate School, where he was later remembered as the man who 'would talk Keats by the

[1] October 1861.   [2] 11 May 1861, p. 629
[3] *Life of James Dixon*, pp. 47–8.

42

hour', but after a short while he fell ill and resigned. He moved, perhaps for the sake of his health, away from London, and in October 1862 took up his duties as Second Master of Carlisle High School. Accounts of his teaching years are slight and fragmentary, but they suggest that he was not temperamentally suited to life in the blackboard jungle. His headmaster at Carlisle recalled

He was really too good and simple minded a man for a schoolmaster. I remember his saying that Prometheus had forgotten the *insani leonis vim* in his composition. He was of course a good scholar and could teach well if anyone wanted to learn, but nature had not given him much of that indescribable power which makes boys feel that it is dangerous to go too far with a man.[1]

And one of his pupils there remembered that

in the afternoon during school, he would sometimes rest his head on his hand and lose himself in thought while a smile bred of musing over pleasant fancies stole across his face. Presently all the boys in the class would have their grinning faces resting on their hands. A splutter from one of them would cause him to look suddenly up and see their game, and he would give a lot of impositions, which however he did not always insist on being done.[2]

In 1863 he published his Oxford Prize Poem on a Sacred Subject, *S. John in Patmos*, which we may regard as an addition to the series of poems in 'Christ's Company'. Like 'St. John' it recounts a mystic's vision with a powerful awareness of the reality of Good and Evil:

> the earth in plague and blight
> Plunged her black form amid the angry light
> From baleful meteors cast, impetuous broke
> On th'upper air 'mid dim sulphureous smoke
> The brood of hell, whose king Abaddon was:
> There was the rush of countless steeds that pass
> To fields of death; the third of men are slain;

[1] T. C. Durham to W. Rees in Bodley MS.,Don.e.20, fol. 43.
[2] H. J. Bulkeley to Rees in Bodley MS.,Don.e.20, fol. 20.

> Yet unrepentant they who still remain:
> Then in this dreariness of blood and shade
> Obscure and monstrous shapes the world invade,
> The Dragon, Beast, False Prophet, cursed three,
> Earth's torturers, infernal trinity: . . .
>
> But now, behold, the triumph comes at last,
> The strife is over and the woes are past;
> The troubled vision ends in glorious rest;
> Time by eternity is dispossessed.

But its imagery is less rich and its colouring more subdued than the earlier poem's now that the Pre-Raphaelite influence in Dixon's work is waning. This even, controlled verse owes less to Rossetti's school than to the work of William Lisle Bowles and Dixon's boyhood favourite, Cowper. In one passage of *S. John in Patmos* it seems that we obtain a glimpse of the poet himself, aware of a conflict between the calls of social duty and of private intellectual joys:

> For they are ever honoured most who lean
> To human wants from out that cloud serene
> Of solemn thought, in which they fain would dwell,
> But that the earth hath need of them to quell
> Its anarchies: they who with burning heart
> Come down their own strong essence to impart,
> And labour noblest things to keep alive:
> True men of action, though contemplative.

The following year saw the publication of *Historical Odes and Other Poems*, a miscellany of historical narratives, religious poems in the 'Christ's Company' series, medieval tales in the 'Crosses of Love' series, reflective odes, eclogues, sonnets and lyrics. Most of this verse is undistinguished. The three 'historical odes', 'Wellington', 'Marlborough' and 'Havelock's March', originally written for a proposed joint volume with Fulford, have a raucous assertiveness that is foreign to Dixon's nature and is not found elsewhere in his work, but 'Sir John Franklin', the fourth of the historical narratives, is better, and rises occasionally from 'prize poem' flatness to nobility and pathos. It was probably Dixon's entry in a special competition in 1860, when a prize of fifty pounds was offered for the best poem by a non-resident member of Oxford University on 'The Life, the Character and the Death of the heroic seaman Sir John Franklin, with special reference to the time, place and discovery of his death.' Swinburne entered the competition too, and, like Dixon, was unsuccessful.[1] Additions to the *Christ's Company* group and 'Love's Consolation' series are unremarkable, except in that the two narratives illustrating Crosses of Love, 'Concealment' and 'Perversity', embody Dixon's view of carnal love as a pitiable misfortune. 'Concealment' captures the note of passionate regret and the all-pervading pathos of its source in the *Heptameron* of Marguerite de Valois; 'Perversity's' story is apparently Dixon's own and is less impressive, for its motive of sheer perversity is more difficult to present convincingly than the pathological melancholia in the other story. Two philosophical eclogues, 'The Birth of Apollo' and 'Orpheus', mark a new, but not highly successful, venture.

The most interesting verse is in the four reflective odes and the miscellaneous shorter poems. In these there is a little Wordsworthian philosophizing and a great deal of word painting which lends weight both to Hopkins's assertion—'Wordpainting is, in the verbal arts, the great success of our day',[2] and to Morris's—'Our clique was much influenced by Keats, who was a poet who represented semblances, as opposed to Shelley who had no eyes.'[3] Dixon's manifestly derivative ode 'To Summer' is one of the better productions of that large Victorian academy of word painting devotees of Keats:

> Thou who dost set the prop to crooked arms
>   Of apple-trees that labour with their store;
> Who givest sunshine to the nestling farms
>   Along the valley, that their roofs may pore
> More placidly upon the open sky;

[1] See G. Lafourcade, *Swinburne, a Literary Biography*, 1932, p. 77.
[2] C. C. Abbott (ed.), *Letters of Gerard Manley Hopkins to Robert Bridges*, 1955, p. 267.
[3] *Collected Works of William Morris*, 1910–15, XXII, xxxi.

Thou who dost bid the poplars swing so high
    Through thy sweet breath, and pourest rustling waves
Of air along the forest-fledged hill;
    Who by the shore dost froth the ocean caves
With green translucent billows, coming still
Till the clear reefs and hollows sob and thrill;
    Imperial summer, thou art nigh;
    Giver of sweetness, thou art come;
Magician of the soul's melodious gloom,
Whisperer of heaven, great queen of poesy.

I see thee lead the weeping morning up,
    That thy bright sun might kiss away her tears;
I see thee drench thy moon in dewy cup,
    Which from the roses Hebe evening bears;
High in the heaven is set thy smouldering tower
Of cloudy watch for many a noontide hour;
    Whence thou descendest on the misty vale
Far off, and in green hollows all thine own
    Leanest thy brow, for loving languor pale,
While some sweet lay of love is let alone,
Or some sweet whisper dies away unknown:
    Then with the sunset thou dost rise,
    And mournfully dost mark
Thy softening clouds subdued into the dark,
The shutting of thy flowers, and thy bereaved skies.

Yet thou must fade, sweet nurse of budded boughs;
    Thy beauty hath the tenderness of death;
Thy fickle sun is riding from thine house;
    Thy perfect fulness waits for withering breath:
Already, see, the broad-leaved sycamore
Drops one by one his honours to the floor:
    For his wide mouths thou canst no longer find,
Poor mother that thou art, the needful food;
    The air doth less abound with nectar kind;
And soon his brethren of the prosperous wood
Shall paler grow; thou shalt be sallow-hued,
    Mother, too soon; dies too
    The aspiration thou hast sent,
The thrilling joy, the sweet content
That live with trees so green and heavens so blue.

This is quite good, but it cannot stand beside 'To Autumn'. Like the young ladies of its day, it is 'pale and interesting'. Dixon has some happy descriptive touches, but his images are on the whole far too imprecise, and his summer quite lacks the sensuous fullness of Keats's autumn. The excessive sweetness, the breath of decay, the 'sob and thrill' and the 'loving languor pale' bring us into the Pre-Raphaelites' world.

Another ode 'Rapture' opens with a word picture in which Dixon paints in the details of middle distance and foreground successively and carefully, as a Holman Hunt or a Ford Madox Brown would:

> The white and crumbling clouds leave bare the blue;
> Shines out the central sun with golden hue;
> And all the fruit-trees, rolling blossom-boughed,
> Are white and billowy as the rolling cloud.
> The warm beam bedded sleeps upon the trees,
> The springing thickets and the gorse-bound leas;
> Sleeps where I lie at ease,
> Pulling the ruby orchis and the pale
> Half-withered cowslip from the hill-side grass,
> Midway the brow that overhangs the vale,
> Where the sleepy shadows pass,
> And the sunbeam sleeps till all is grown
> Into one burning sapphire stone,
> All air, all earth, each violet-deepened zone.
>
> It sleeps and broods upon the moss-mapped stone,
> The thready mosses and the plumy weeds;
> Numbers the veined flowers one after one . . .

But this ode is noteworthy too as an account of a mystical experience. Dixon tells, not without 'obscurities of expression which are of themselves and not through the reader's want of apprehension faulty',[1] how he looks through the appearances of natural objects to the metaphysical reality behind them. He becomes aware through his senses of 'A

---

[1] Hopkins in a letter to Dixon, *Correspondence*, p. 36.

soul occult in Nature, hidden deep' which is the unity
underlying diversity that all mystics seek to know:

> Like to a dream,
> Through sense and all by sense conveyed,
> Into our soul the shadow of that soul
> Doth float.
> Then are we lifted up erect and whole
> In vast confession to that universe
> Perceived by us: our soul itself transfers
> Thither by instinct sure; it swiftly hails
> The mighty spirit similar.

Dixon sees into the life of things, he finds that the soul of
Nature is God's love, and he goes on to tell how the human
soul offers love to God who embraces it in his own love.
'Rapture' is full of religious good intentions but does not
quite succeed in communicating and elucidating a religious
experience. Bridges, perhaps rightly, dismissed it as a
'flagrant example' of philosophizing in Wordsworth's
manner, for, unhappily, the mystical vision—in the vague,
abstract terms in which Dixon describes it—appears syn-
thetic rather than spontaneous. Nevertheless we have no
reason to disbelieve that Dixon did enjoy in a certain
moment of concentration and happiness some experience,
arising from a harmony between his religious intuitions and
his sensations of the outside world, of the kind that is
adumbrated in this poem, and that the unease expressed in
much of his later verse may stem partly from his belief that
this experience would not be repeated.

With 'Rapture' we may associate the sonnet 'Humanity'
which proclaims once again Dixon's belief in mystical unity,
here seen in the light of the Neo-Platonic doctrine of emana-
tion—that the souls of individual men proceed from and
return to the World Soul and share its nature. This sound
piece of sonneteering is deservedly popular among antholo-
gists. The 'Spirit of the Sphere', though in no sense a
philosophical poem, is based upon the same conception of
the spiritual oneness of life. It is an invocation to the,
unidentified, joyful presence indwelling in all natural things.

The remarkable 'Inscience' perhaps laments the fading of a quasi-mystical vision, but more probably it expresses Dixon's regret at the ending of his intense intellectual and emotional life within the Brotherhood. This poem, a romantic's cry for his own lost Golden Age, communicates directly by an other-worldly symbolism its author's past 'meteorosophia' and present despair:

> The wind, like mist of purple grain,
> Arises o'er the Arab plain;
> Strange constellations flashing soar
> Above the dreadful Boreal shore.
>
> But never purple cloud I see
> Swelling above immensity;
> And never galaxy doth peer
> Through the thick mists that wrap me here:
> Hard is the way, shut is the gate,
> And life is in a narrow strait.
> Once only did my soul aspire
> To scale the Orient dropping fire;
> Once only floated in the ways
> Of heaven apart from earthly haze:
> And then it was a foolish soul,
> And knew not how the heavens do roll.

In its smaller number of pages *Historical Odes* embraces a wider field of forms and subjects than the 1861 volume. Even after we have set aside the 'historical odes', stories of Crosses of Love and additions to 'Christ's Company', all of which may be considered as parts of larger schemes outside this book, we are left with a miscellany. Nevertheless some of the shorter poems have in common the quality of tender pathos and the theme of a faded vision, while Dixon's own idiom may be heard in them from time to time. We hear his characteristic plaintive note in *Mercy*,

> Earth, sad earth, thou roamest
> Through the day and night;
> Weary with the darkness,
> Weary with the light.

> Clouds of hanging judgment,
>> And the cloud that weeps for me,
> Swell above the mountain,
>> Strive above the sea,
>
> But, sad earth, thou knowest
>> All my love for thee;
> Therefore thou dost welcome
>> The cloud that weeps for me,

in the well-known 'Song',—

> The feathers of the willow
> Are half of them grown yellow
>> Above the swelling stream;
> And ragged are the bushes,
> And rusty now the rushes,
>> And wild the clouded gleam.
>
> The thistle now is older,
> His stalk begins to moulder,
> His head is white as snow;
> The branches all are barer,
> The linnet's song is rarer,
>> The robin pipeth now,

in the last stanza of 'To Summer' (p. 46 above) and in these
opening lines from 'Ode on Departing Youth',

> His icicle upon the frozen bough
> Stern winter hangs, where hung the leaf ere now:
> In soft diffusion doth the morning creep
> Along the clouded heaven from mound to mound,
> So faint and wan, the woods are still asleep,
> And pallid shadows scarcely mark the ground.
>
> Then comes the thought, Alas that summer dies;
> Alas that youth should melancholy grow
> In waning hours, and lose the alchemies
> That make its thickest clouds with gold to glow!

Dixon delicately personalizes common observed natural
phenomena and links them with his own emotional states

50

in one sad autumnal mood. He projects his own feelings of regret and resignation upon the objects he describes and, in 'To Summer' and 'On Departing Youth', explicitly compares nature's decay with the failing of youthful aspirations. It is a fault in these two odes that he should declare his feelings alongside his images rather than through them, and so make his poetic statements diffuse where they should be concentrated; in the 'Song', the least self conscious of all the poems in *Historical Odes*, there is something closer to a total fusion of emotion and object.

Historical Odes contains some writing of a high order, but, like *Christ's Company*, includes much work that should have been left unpublished. The reviewers again slew the bad poems and interred the good with them, and Dixon's book was as generally ignored by readers as the earlier had been. Dixon continued to write verse but after the discouraging reception of *Historical Odes* he became less eager to rush into print. He wrote to Hatch in 1866—

> As for me my history is comprised in the following sentence: School will re-open tomorrow Aug 14. Not altogether though. I have other things in me besides school work. I stick to poetry & ever shall. My intersticial time is given up to that.
>
> I have got a long poem nearly ready for press, & also nearly a volume of shorter ones. I do not however mean to publish for at least a year.
>
> It is little use publishing unless one can also advertise largely, & at present this is quite out of my power. I hope that my mind is not at a standstill.

The long poem was probably the 'Northern Epic' which Dixon later destroyed. It was begun before Morris's Northern tales in verse—'most of it was written before he began Jason, much more the Earthly Paradise'[1]—and was based upon some Northern myth, possibly the Twilight of the Gods, since Bridges thought that it too closely resembled *Hyperion*.

By 1868, when Dixon left the High School to become a

---

[1] *Correspondence*, p. 45, see also p. 37.

minor canon and Honorary Librarian of Carlisle Cathedral, he had indefinitely postponed the publication of more verse. He turned instead to history and made his first serious study of the sixteenth-century Church while preparing an article on the English Liturgy for a projected encyclopaedia. The plans for the encyclopaedia fell through, but he continued his work and announced that he had 'In Preparation: *A History of the Book of Common Prayer, and other Authorized Formularies of the Church of England from the time of the separation from Rome.*' This work was mentioned in a letter to Hatch on 10 July 1873—'I am pushing on my Hist. of the Prayer Book, which will I think contain some interesting discoveries.' Like the encyclopaedia article it was never published, but its material was eventually used in Dixon's monumental *History of the Church of England* which was begun in 1874.

On 28 December 1871 James Dixon died, well over eighty but preserving his intellectual vigour to the end. The Methodists considered that his prominence in their movement justified a *Life* and called upon Richard to provide it. So he wrote rather hastily in the first half of 1873 his *Life of James Dixon, D.D., Wesleyan Minister* and it was published in the following year. The book gives an admirably generous and affectionate account of James Dixon's public life and of the movement he served, but, disappointingly, contains little information about the Dixon family and Richard himself. However there may be self-revelation in this passage:

How many a poor minister of the Established Church, flung down for life on some bare hill-side, or in some unlettered hamlet, far from books, far from all intercourse that may tend to cheer and freshen his spiritual life, has reason to lament that something like the Methodist itinerancy is not embraced in the ecclesiastical system to which he belongs.[1]

Carlisle Cathedral and Library did not constitute an unlettered hamlet, nevertheless Dixon may have been obliquely

---

[1] *Life of James Dixon*, p. 467.

lamenting his own case, for he had found nothing in middle age to replace the freshening intercourse of the Oxford Brotherhood. He met the members of the Set rarely and corresponded only intermittently with them, but still, at forty, he idealized his old friendships and wrote to the Brothers with the affection and in the idiom of their youth, as this letter to Price bears out:

Grange-over-Sands . . .
25 July 1873

My dear Crom,

Many thanks for thy kind congratulations,[1] for which I was looking; for all the sneeshin' I have had seemed imperfect without thy mull. Not that you have made a mull of it, but in thinking too much of my success. Here I am with Wife and Daughter enjoying as sweet a place for holiday as is to be found in England, while you I presume are still at the delightful (= a new addition to the stock of the rosy, the balmy &c: 'delightful task to rear &c.' who said it? Thomson?) The address on your letter reminds me how long it is since I saw you: long enough for me to have gone to a new house & lived in it for three years—it is now *4 George S. Carlisle*, where a bed is at your service whenever you will come.

I heard from Faulkner the day that he and Morris went off to Iceland, and hope to see them on their way home in September. From Fulford too I heard the other day, but nothing about himself: he is however at the same place where he was when last I was in London. When shall I be in London again? No prospect of it at present: and I seem partly to have lost the wish to see it again. It seemed so changed last time—or am I so changed that I hardly knew it. Among my unpublished remains is a satire on the subject.

It is so long since I wrote the Essay, that I had all but forgotten it, (sent—in Aug '72—adjudged July 3 '73), when I got news of the prize. Of course I am very glad of it. Since I wrote it, I have written my Father's Life, which will be published I hope

---

[1] On Dixon's winning second prize in the Peek Essay Competition. H. W. Peek was an M.P., opposed to disestablishment of the Church of England, who had announced in July 1871 that he would give prizes of £400, £200 and £100 for the three best essays on 'The Maintenance of the Church of England as an Established Church.'

shortly. You saw him once in London in company with Hatch, I remember, and you talked Darwinism.

I have heard from Hatch lately, who is or was at Glenalmond College near Perth examining. I have no other news of men: but should be glad to hear any—e.g. of Hill, who is probably going on in his quiet path of duty and above all of Ned. from whom I never hear by any chance.

I should enormously like to have a meeting of some of the old set: but suppose that this is not to be. Let me hear sometime soon, & believe me,

My dear Crom,
Ever thine . . .[1]

But a year later a meeting of some of the old Set did take place, and on 18 August 1874 Dixon wrote to Price again:

I saw Ted and Morris at the abode of splendour last week— slept there, and we were most jolly. Ned is in poor health, I grieve to find, and a little quieter in manner—otherwise un-altered. Topsy genial, gentle, delightful; both full of affection: it was a most happy meeting; would you had been there.

yours for ever and ever . . .[2]

The abode of splendour was Naworth Castle, the home of George Howard later Earl of Carlisle, and its splendour was augmented shortly after this happy meeting by the decorative work of Morris and Burne-Jones. Dixon was a frequent visitor there.

His published verse of ten years and more ago was still neglected by the reading public but it was not entirely unappreciated. On 26 May 1875 Dante Gabriel Rossetti wrote to him:

Is it a compliment or the contrary to tell a man whom one has known for 18 years that one had no idea till now of his possessing first rate powers? At any rate I must confess that such is the sentence that comes uppermost in beginning this letter, after the great enjoyment of reading your poems.

By what inexcusable accident I never read them before, I cannot now tell, but there is only one impression possible now on

---

[1] Bodley MS.,Don.e.20, fol. 88.
[2] *Memorials of Burne-Jones*, ii. 50, Mackail, *Life of Morris*, i. 304.

54

doing so: viz: that you are one of the most subtle as well as varied of our poets, and that the neglect of such work as yours on all hands is an incomprehensible accident.

There is so much that is admirable, and in such different kinds, among your poems that it is not easy to make a summary of one's opinion of them. Perhaps in the first volume the most noteworthy things are the description of the vision in 'St. John' and the greater part of the beautiful piece called 'Love's Consolation' except indeed that the conclusion of this latter (in common with some others of yours) seems rather hurried and neglected. The metre adopted in 'St. John' and 'La Faerie' is to me a new variation on that class of stanza. Is it your own? It is very happily contrived. In the second volume there is a visible deepening of motive, though the attempt to make poetry out of modern stories (when so much is commercial in origin and mechanical in means) is, while irresistible to a wide-minded poet, hardly ever quite successful.

Franklin is certainly a noble subject, and several pages of your poem—notably the opening lines and the grand burst of feeling from 'They saw the northern miracles' to 'who died so well', are thoroughly worthy of so great a theme. I prefer the 'Marlborough' to the 'Wellington' which latter seems to me to be in need of condensation & on the whole a subject really more suited to a prose verdict than to a poetical one; though I remember I did not fail to write my own Wellington Funeral poem like other rhymesters. I think the 'Orpheus' on the whole the finest of all your poems, the description of music at pages 101, 102, truly profound and exquisite. Here again however most untowardly the close seems to need further development to make it worthy of the rest.

The close of the very fine ode 'Rapture' seems to me also at fault: slight metres can hardly follow sustained ones without needing, as it were, an organ burst at the close to bring the melody to its full. But this, as well as the 2 Odes 'To Summer' & 'On Departing Youth' delighted me greatly. 'Perversity' is a very well characterized & developed story: 'Concealment' seems to me much weaker, though it contains one line—

'And in that noon joy's shadow falls both ways'

which is among the very finest I know.

Many thanks (though tardy ones) my dear Dixon, for so much good work. Surely there must be more in store by this time, & no one will be better pleased to read it in due season than myself.

With very kind remembrances,
Ever truly yours,
D. G. Rossetti

P.S. I have not seen Ned Jones very lately but my impression is that he has certainly been much better as a rule than he was six or nine months back. The last time I saw him, he seemed well.

Dixon replied on 6 June 1875:

It has been impossible for me to reply before now to your letter on my Poems. I never received and assuredly never expected to have received such a letter. All that I can say in reply to the commendation which is bestowed in it is that I would rather have that letter than all the laudations of all the periodicals in existence. Of the two parts into which the world is divided, work doing and fault finding, I consider that the latter is far worse performed than the former. My work has met with nearly absolute neglect, but along with this there has been some censure of a very ignorant sort. Your approbation makes up for everything.

As to your admirable criticism I agree with it all: and am particularly pleased that you have singled out Orpheus which nobody in public or private has ever spoken of. You are also the only person who has detected the Stanza of St. John and La Faerie, which is a variation of my own on the old seven versed stanza. I have most doubt in my own mind about the tales in verse and had come to conclude that I could not narrate, so what you say has encouraged me. I had designed to have nine tales illustrating causes of failure in love, Love's Consolation to be the Prologue, but it is difficult to get stories of a typical sort. As yet I have only one story unpublished to add to those in the books. I have several volumes of poems in MS: but no immediate prospect of publishing. I can hardly yet believe that I have received so much commendation from the author of The Staff & Scrip, The Burden of Nineveh, and Stratton Water: whom I have always regarded as the greatest master of thought and art in the world.

> Believe me,
> My dear Rossetti,
> Yours always
> R. W. Dixon.

P.S. I have just been presented to a small living, not far from Naworth: and shall be moving thither in a few months.

4

Hayton and *Mano*

Dixon's small living, to which he moved towards the end of 1875, was Hayton, about seven miles east of Carlisle. Its church building, dating from 1780, was plain, but the view from the churchyard was extensive and beautiful. Eastwards the Cumberland fells were quite close; far away to the south-west, in full view, were the mountains of the Lake District, with Saddleback, Skiddaw and Helvellyn prominent; while to the north were the Scottish hills. Near by, the Eden valley made a picturesque landscape, with murmuring river, steep wooded banks, watch-tower, caves, castle, old church and ruined priory. The many local antiquities included Hadrian's Wall—which Dixon had to protect from time to time against Cumberland farmers in search of building materials for their byres and pigsties.

The vicarage establishment at Hayton comprised Mrs. Dixon, two of the daughters—Louisa and Jessie (the third, Emily, was away working as a governess)—servants, a pony (bought from the previous incumbent), many cats and a large black retriever dog which, according to a villager, was fed with port wine. Dixon's new parishioners saw a tallish, stooping middle-aged man, short-necked, with a crest of grey hair and short goat-like beard, a well-shaped aquiline nose and large, kind, but mournful, water-grey eyes. People commented on his facial resemblance in middle age to Chaucer as he appears in the Hoccleve portrait, and the likeness, we know, went deeper, extending to the gifts of acute powers of observation and a kindly ironic humour. He was described as a slow, deliberate and clear speaker, and a sympathetic, attentive listener. His chronic ill health was betrayed by his slow step, bronchial wheezings and a stoop. During his eight years in the parish he was respected and well liked by the villagers who only dimly realized that he did other, scholarly and literary work. He was a devoted pastor, but, unlike his father, not an impressive preacher. His sermons were long, notoriously learned and often above the heads of most of his auditors. Many, reflecting perhaps his Methodist upbringing, impressed upon his hearers the duty of self-examination. He chose mournful and penitential hymns. In conversation his ironic humour and invariable self-depreciation puzzled his parishioners who could comprehend little of his whole nature but loved him for his great kindness of heart.

At Hayton he continued his *History of the Church of England from the Abolition of the Roman Jurisdiction*, begun at Carlisle. This work was planned and executed upon a massive scale and, in view of Dixon's parochial duties and his distance from good libraries, its successful completion, in six volumes covering the period 1529 to 1570, showed remarkable courage, determination and intellectual stamina. While writing it he was continually made aware of his disadvantages, and the work went forward with painful slowness. At the end of the first year's labours he wrote in his diary

An historian may not plead difficulties, but if he might, I could: want of books leading to constant corrections and insertions of newly found matter, remote situation, many interruptions! But who has a right to expect less than every possible difficulty?[1]

The troubles of 1876 were further weighted by the death of his wife. Owing to the scantiness of records she appears in

---

[1] H. Gee, Preface to R. W. Dixon's *History of the Church of England*, vol. v, 1902, p. x.

Dixon's biography as a far more shadowy figure than her importance deserves. Her death may have occasioned that delicate twilight elegy 'O Ubi? Nusquam' (see p. 116 below).

The first volume of Dixon's *History of the Church of England,* carrying the narrative from 1529 to 1537, was completed in spring 1877 and published at the beginning of the following year. Lacking an introduction to explain its purpose and scope, the *History* did not immediately capture attention. Indeed, Dixon's stature as an ecclesiastical historian was not recognized until the third volume was issued seven years later. The publication of this first volume left him out of pocket and the reviewers gave no more than mild encouragement, but he went on to write the second volume, during the course of which he described, not without self-mockery, John Leland:

> This unhappy man, a clergyman, one of that inexplicable race who haunt old libraries, crawl round mouldering walls, dwell among tombs, and for no earthly advantage lose their youth, their eyes, their nerves, in poring over the various relics of departed ages: who hold a life to be well spent in clearing an inscription or rectifying a date: who maintain that what is old is venerable: and who sometimes publish a book at the cost of their substance, that they may preserve some portion of the past from the devouring vitality of the present . . .[1]

Dixon continued to write poetry while engaged upon the *History,* and his long narrative poem *Mano* was produced wholly or in part during his first three or four years at Hayton. Discouraging circumstances attended its writing, as Robert Bridges tells:

> Fearing that the isolation of his clerical routine at Hayton was weaning him from the effort of composition, he determined to bind himself to write at least one canto of this epic every month and bring it with him to the monthly clerical meeting to deposit with a brother parson, whose confidence and sympathy were assured. He punctually executed his task—I cannot say over how long a time it extended—and on the day when he

[1] *History of the Church of England,* vol. ii, 1881, p. 354.

brought the final canto . . . he then for the first time ventured to inquire of his friend what opinion he had formed of the poem. He found that his friend had never had the curiosity to read a line of it; so he took his sheaves home with him, and garnered them in his cupboard with other poems and epics that slept on the shelf gathering grime.[1]

His wife was dead, his early friends far away and his poetry unread. Melancholy could not be fended off entirely by his work on the *History*. So it must have seemed providential when in June 1878 he received from Gerard Manley Hopkins, a former pupil of his at Highgate and now a Jesuit priest, an unexpected letter full of delicate, understanding praise of his neglected verses:

to shew you how greatly I prized them, when I entered my present state of life, in which I knew I could have no books of my own . . . I copied out *St. Paul, St. John, Love's Consolation,* and others from both volumes and keep them by me. . . . I knew what I should feel myself in your position—if I had written and published works the extreme beauty of which the author himself the most keenly feels and they had fallen out of sight at once and been (you will not mind my saying it, as it is, I suppose, plainly true) almost wholly unknown; then, I say, I should feel a certain comfort to be told they had been deeply appreciated by some one person, a stranger, at all events and had not been published quite in vain. . . .

I have said all this, and could if there were any use say more, as a sort of duty of charity to make up, so far as one voice can do, for the disappointment you must, at least at times, I think, have felt over your rich and exquisite work almost thrown away.[2]

Dixon was deeply moved, 'shaken to the very centre', by Hopkins's generous praise, and a friendship sprang up between the two men which continued until Hopkins's death in 1889 and was of great comfort for both. Hopkins introduced Dixon to Robert Bridges whose published verse, tiny in quantity and flawless in execution, was known in 1878 to few readers, and the three men formed a close circle of

---

[1] *Selected Poems,* pp. xxvii, xxviii.   [2] *Correspondence,* pp. 1, 2, 3.

hidden poets, helping each other with encouragement and criticism. For Dixon his two new friends constituted a second Brotherhood. Once again 'the bond was poetry'.

Bridges had at first what he described as 'humiliating' difficulty in appreciating Dixon's poems. Nine years after Dixon's death he wrote:

> Such a poem as *Inscience*, of which now I feel as if I could hardly praise enough, did not when I first read it make any impression on me at all . . . appreciation came very slowly: and had it not been for 'The Feathers of the Willow' I should not (when first I saw the poems) have suspected Dixon's powers.[1]

Dixon thought highly of Bridges's verse from the first, but reserved his greatest praise for Hopkins's. He was not put off by its strangeness, as most Victorian readers would have been, but saw at once what a rare and true gift of poetry his friend possessed. Bridges and Patmore, who constituted with Dixon the entire audience for Hopkins's poetry, preferred those poems that were least characteristic of their author but were closest to what Patmore called 'the ordinary rules of composition'. Patmore wrote 'I do not think that I could ever become sufficiently accustomed to your favourite Poem, "The Wreck of the Deutschland" to reconcile me to its strangenesses.'[2] Hopkins had to plead with Bridges to read it twice. But Dixon readily appreciated its enormous power and enjoyed too, the other strange and original poems of Hopkins—those which 'could have been written by none other'. His reaction on first reading some of Hopkins's manuscripts in April 1879 was characteristically impulsive and generous. He wrote 'I have your Poems and have read them I cannot say with what delight, astonishment, and admiration. . . . It seems to me that they ought to be published. Can I do anything?'[3]—and then suggested that, to awaken public interest, he should mention them in an 'abrupt footnote' to his account of the Jesuit Society in his *Church History*. When this offer was declined he asked

[1] Bodley MS.,Eng.Lett.d.143, fol. 56.
[2] C. C. Abbott (ed.), *Further Letters of G. M. Hopkins*, 1956, p. 353.
[3] *Correspondence*, pp. 26, 27.

permission to send 'The Loss of the Eurydice' for publication in a Carlisle newspaper, and aroused a fluttered refusal from Hopkins.

When he returned the manuscripts in March the following year he made an acute comment upon the effect of Hopkins's poetry—'in the power of forcibly and delicately giving the essence of things in nature, and of carrying one out of one's self with healing, these poems are unmatched'.[1] Hopkins, who needed encouragement 'as the crops need water', was cheered and stimulated by such criticism, while Dixon was happy in discovering the gifts of his new friend. He was happy too in his own work. He completed the second volume of the *History* more easily and quickly than the first, and then turned back to poetry with the encouragement of his new friends and under the stimulus of a visit to Hayton by Bridges in summer 1880. Bridges described the visit in his *Memoir* of Dixon:

it was by train that I arrived one afternoon, and first saw Dixon awaiting me on the platform of How Mill station. Emotion graved the scene on my memory: a tallish, elderly figure, its litheness lost in a slight, scholarly stoop which gave to the shoulders an appearance of heaviness, wearing unimpeachable black cloth negligently, and a low-crowned clerical hat banded with twisted silk. His attitude and gait as he walked on the platform were those of a man who, through abstraction or indifference, is but half aware of his surroundings, and his attention to the train as he gazed along the carriages to discover me had that sort of awkwardness that comes from the body not expressing the intention of the mind. His face, I saw, was dark and solemn, and as he drew near I could see that the full lips gave it a tender expression, for the beard did not hide the mouth. Nothing further could be read, only the old mystery and melancholy of the earth, and that under the heavy black brows his eyes did their angelic service to the soul without distraction. His hearty welcome was in a voice that startled me with its sonority and depth; but in its convincing sincerity there was nothing expansive or avenant. He then became so silent that I

---

[1] *Correspondence*, p. 32.

half suspected him of common tactics, and was slow to interpret his silence as mere courtesy, which it was; indeed, he would never speak unless he were assured that he was not preventing another, a habit which made a singularly untrue disguise of his eager, ingenuous temper. . . .

The characteristic of Dixon which was most outwardly apparent was his humility. With many it passed for shyness or gaucherie, whereas he was at his ease in any company, with sympathy and observation both actively engaged. This modesty was entirely natural, and so excessive as to reach the pitch where modest manners assume distinction. . . .

He was then a widower, living with his two grown-up step-daughters a simple life full of professional engagements. The domestic round closed early, and he and I would then repair to his study upstairs, and chat by the unseasonable but comforting fire until the small hours. Like his father he was a clerical smoker indoors, and, I think, valued the use of tobacco too much to count it a luxury. His pipe lay on his writing-table in careless brotherhood with his old quill pens. Of the many nights spent thus, I can recall little but the inexhaustible pleasure of our conversation, and the reluctance with which we dutifully separated for our beds. He had many poems to show, and I could read them with the excitement which the likelihood of discovering treasure always brings. His muse, too, was then new to me, and its strangeness drew our unencumbered discourse far afield. Those nights I remember better than the days, of which, however, some distinct pictures remain: one is of Dixon's favourite walk in a deep combe, where the trees grew thickly and a little stream flowed by the foundations of old Roman masonry; another is a game of lawn-tennis—it could have no other name, for only the implements of that game or their approximate substitutes were used. The scene after thirty years is undimmed; I am standing with Dixon and two ladies in the bright sunlight on a small plot of grass surrounded by high laurestinus bushes in full flower, and crossed by festoons of light netting. I am more spectator than player, lazily from time to time endeavouring to place a ball where Dixon might be likely to reach it, or mischievously screwing it in order to perplex him. He like a terrier after a rat, as if there were nothing else in the world, in such rapturous earnestness that I wonder we did not play oftener. He was not, even at school, much given to games, and only the tennis-racquet betrayed to me, what few of his most intimate friends knew, that he was left-handed.[1]

Bridges urged Dixon to publish some of his accumulated verse, and wrote on 11 August to Henry Daniel to suggest that the Daniel Press should print a small anthology of the verse of Bridges and four friends, including Dolben, Hopkins and Dixon ('who once published unsuccessfully but is sure of his position, surer in my estimation than Morris himself'). This scheme fell through but Dixon was anthologized elsewhere. In 1880 Hall Caine was compiling a Sonnet Anthology and Rossetti wrote to him:

> There is an admirable but totally unknown living poet named Dixon. I will send you two small vols. of his which he gave me long ago, but please take good care of them, and return them as soon as done with. I value them highly. . . .
>
> He should certainly be represented in your book. If I live, I mean to write something about him in some quarter when I can. His finest passages are as fine as any living man can do. . . . If you wanted to ask him for an original sonnet you might mention my name.[2]

Dixon contributed to the anthology 'Give me the darkest corner of a cloud', 'Humanity' and a new sonnet 'Perished Ideals', which is remarkable only for its eldritch rime scheme.[3]

He was now sending his manuscripts to Hopkins and Bridges. In January 1881 he sent a bundle of poems to Hopkins, asking for 'any observations or corrections that occur to you', and sent to Bridges 'Apollo Pythias', a new poem written since his visit, adding in his letter 'I heard from Hopkins this morning; sending two of his sweetly terrible poems.[4] There is something in his work which

---

[1] *Selected Poems*, pp. xix, xx; xxv; xxi, xxii.

[2] T. Hall Caine, *Recollections of D. G. Rossetti*, 1882, p. 258.

[3] abbab cc debde ff (abb abc cde bde ff?). Hopkins said of other, more conventional sonnets by Dixon 'when one goes so far as to run the rhymes of the octet into the sestet a downright prolapsus or hernia takes place and the sonnet is crippled for life'. (*Correspondence*, p. 72.) As far as I know, Hopkins made no diagnosis of 'Perished Ideals'.

[4] 'Brothers' and 'Spring and Fall: to a young child', see *Correspondence*, p. 174.

always makes my heart ache.' The second volume of the *Church History* had received a lukewarm reception. Dixon had bouts of depression; in letters he referred to melancholy fits and to being 'mentally unshipped' and in his diary he noted:

The life of utter solitude is telling on my spirits and manners. Never to speak to a man, unless a villager, from week to week, and month to month! At best to see but another clergyman in a formal official sort of way—this is enough to transform one to a Caliban.[1]

If so, it was a quizzical Caliban who wrote to Bridges:

There has been a man preaching a Lenten sermon here this evening who said—'The trumpet will blow, and you will sail down the river to the rocks where you will sp-br-sbreak'. He then hit the pulpit violently. That man has only been ordained a priest three weeks: and he has done more than I already.

The observations upon his poems that Dixon had asked for fill seven long letters by Hopkins between April and October 1881 and display great care and sympathetic insight. Dixon's briefer replies consist largely of self-depreciation and of criticism of well-known writers of the day, but contain one critical remark upon Hopkins's poems that has become 'canonical'. This was provoked by Dixon's fear that his friend might renounce poetry on entering the Jesuit Second Noviceship:

I hope that you are going on with poetry yourself. I can understand that your present position, seclusion and exercises would give to your writings a rare charm—they have done so in those that I have seen: something that I cannot describe, but know to myself by the inadequate word *terrible pathos*—something of what you call temper in poetry: a right temper which goes to the point of the terrible; the terrible crystal.[2]

---

[1] Gee, Preface to Dixon's *History*, vol. v, pp. xii, xiii.

[2] *Correspondence*, p. 80. Mrs. E. E. Duncan-Jones has shown (*Notes and Queries*, June 1956, p. 257) that 'terrible crystal' occurs at Ezekiel, i. 22 (A.V.): 'And the likeness of the firmament upon the heads of the living creatures was as the colour of the terrible crystal, stretched forth over their heads above.' It seems likely that Dixon used the phrase in this Biblical

Hopkins's reply, declaring that 'the waste of time the very compositions you admire may have caused and their pre-occupation of the mind which belonged to more sacred or more binding duties', and 'the disquiet and the thoughts of vainglory they have given rise to'[1] were incompatible with his dedication to God, aroused an anguished outburst from Dixon:

My dear, dear friend,—Your letter touches & moves me more than I can say. I ought not in your present circumstances tease you with the regret that much of it gives me: to hear of your having destroyed poems & feeling that you have a vocation in comparison of which poetry & the fame that might assuredly be yours is nothing. I could say much, for my heart bleeds: but I ought also to feel the same: and do not as I ought, though I thought myself very indifferent as to fame. So I will say nothing, but cling to the hope that you will find it consistent with all that you have undertaken to pursue poetry still, as occasion may serve: & that in doing so you may be sanctioned & encouraged by the great Society to which you belong, which has given so many ornaments to literature. Surely one vocation cannot destroy another: and such a Society as yours will not remain ignorant that you have such gifts as have seldom been given by God to man.[2]

Although he had said that one vocation cannot destroy another, he was well aware of the dilemma and of the correctness of Hopkins's attitude. In Hopkins the clash of vocations was violent because his highly individualized and self-searching poetry was essentially an art of the 'egotistical

---

sense, that is the sense in which Gilfillan had used it when writing of Cowper—'Thus far he is a minor Ezekiel, in the energy of his appeals, in his vehement denunciations, and in his towering flights towards the "terrible crystal".' (G. Gilfillan, *Poetical Works of William Cowper*, 1854, ii. xii.) If this is so, Dixon criticized better than he knew, for 'crystal' in the sense of chemical crystal, with suggestions of aggregation and concentration, exactly hits off Hopkins's peculiar diamond-hard fusion of passion and form. 'His output was restricted, but at the same time intensified—allotropised from graphite to diamond . . . in the stringency of his "bleak asceticism".' (W. H. Gardner, *Gerard Manley Hopkins, a Study*, vol. i, 1948, p. 37.)

[1] *Correspondence*, p. 88.   [2] *Id.*, pp. 89, 90.

sublime', while Jesuit discipline demanded a complete sub-
mergence of self. Dixon's circumstances were different, but
his introspective, religious nature was not unlike Hopkins's,
and about ten years later he was to be torn by a broadly
similar conflict between the two vocations. Dixon was
always in a position to appreciate Hopkins's spiritual
struggles. That is why he is such an understanding critic of
Hopkins's poems.

One of his letters to Hopkins in October 1881 carried the
postscript 'I ought to tell you that I am engaged to be
married some time or other',[1] and on 9 February 1882 he
was married to Matilda Routledge, the publisher's eldest
daughter, a highly capable woman who was about six years
younger than Dixon. By this marriage, as by his first, he
had no children, but his stepdaughters Louisa and Jessie
Thomson continued to live at home and a niece of his wife
joined the household.

On 27 March he met Hopkins for the first time since
Highgate. Hopkins could spare only a few hours between
trains at Carlisle, which did not give Dixon time to over-
come his shyness, and so the meeting was something of a
disappointment for Hopkins. Shortly afterwards D. G.
Rossetti's death deeply distressed Dixon, and the affection
he had for the master of his Pre-Raphaelite apprenticeship
shines through his contribution to Hall Caine's biographical
sketch published in that year. Dixon now began to make
plans to publish his long poem *Mano* and a volume of those
shorter poems most highly praised by Hopkins and Bridges.
He was working on the reign of Edward VI in the *Church
History* and only giving 'off days' to the revision of *Mano*,
but the historical labours were lightened by the help of
Bridges, who searched out on his instructions pieces of
information in the Record Office and the British Museum.
He still visited London three or four times a year to make
his own investigations and called on Bridges when he did
so. All his literary activities had to be fitted into a closely
limited amount of leisure time, for he did not neglect his

---

[1] *Correspondence*, p. 82.

parochial work or his diocesan duties as rural dean and examining chaplain to his bishop. However the revision of *Mano* was at last completed and the poem published in the summer of 1883.

Mano, a Poetical History: of the Time of the Close of the Tenth Century: concerning the Adventures of a Norman Knight: which fell part in Normandy part in Italy consists of four books divided into short cantos of lengths varying between 40 and 240 verses, making up a total of 5,600 verses. It is written in *terza rima*. The story is invented and most of the characters are invented too, but some are historical—the most notable of these historical figures being the scholar Gerbert who became Pope Sylvester II in 999.

Mano, a knight of mysterious parentage and a protégé of Gerbert, is one of the Norman warriors who, under Count Thurold, are fighting the Saracens in Italy. He returns to the Norman court to gather more men, and with him travels Thurold's daughter Diantha who secretly hates him. In Normandy he falls in love with Blanche who is already betrothed and rejects him, while he in turn is loved by Blanche's sister Joanna. Joanna and Mano independently tell Gerbert of their loves. Gerbert promises to aid Joanna but he conceals her love from Mano because he wishes to retain him as a dependant in his own service. From the same motive Gerbert has hidden from the knight the secret of his noble parentage. Meanwhile Diantha has escaped from Mano's guardianship and gone to live in the forest with her lover and his crew of outlaws. Mano returns to the wars and during his journey is misled by a fiend in woman's shape to help unknowingly in the murder of his own twin sister. For a year he fights under Thurold until the Normans gain great successes; then he comes to Rome where Gerbert, now Pope, honours him. He chivalrously but rashly undertakes an act of revenge on behalf of the daughter of the rebel Laurentius; by doing so he offends Gerbert and is disgraced. Thereupon he returns to Normandy, having promised Thurold that he will find Diantha and restore her to him. He finds her among the rebel peasants and outlaws, but at that moment the followers of the vicious Robert, Archbishop of Rouen, attack, and Mano, attempting to bring Diantha out of the fight, kills one of Robert's knights. The Archbishop assumes that Mano was consorting with rebels and condemns him and Diantha to death. Meanwhile Joanna, in the convent where Gerbert had sent her, has discovered Mano's true parentage. She reveals to Robert that Mano is his half-brother, but he will not believe her. She comes to the castle where the two prisoners await execution, assists Diantha's escape and takes her place. Joanna and Mano are killed together just after they have discovered their mutual love.

These adventures take place in a world awaiting the Millennium and daily expecting its own dissolution, so the events described in the poem take on a strange portentousness. As Dixon had declared in his prefatory address 'To the Reader':

> Wherefore, as in the sunset's reddening glare
> The shapes of earth stand stronger on the sky,
> So saw I life enhanced, as it were,
>   And lifted in that light of misery:
> And thought to set my thoughts of man's estate
> The better in those colours wild and high:
>   To track the dark intricate coils of Fate,
> The infinite of pain, the brief of joy,
> The better round that far and mystic date.

The tale begins in a sombre mood and a low tone, as Fergant the narrator introduces himself and describes the crumbling hillsides that image man's mortality,

> I, Fergant, living now my latest days,
> Gerbert's disciple once, but long a monk
> Of Sant Evreult, for that in many ways
>   I have beheld God's strokes upon the trunk
> Of rotten trees: and seen the cedars tall
> Fall on the hills, because the earth has shrunk
>   From nourishing, herself washed down by fall
> Of pelting rains, and crumbled by the sun,

70

So that no state may be perpetual:
    And knowing how things dwindle one by one
To him who clings to this world's misery
Some longer while, ere to the grave he run:
    I, looking soon for that; and since that I
Have seen some things that shall not happen twice,
And days return not that be once gone by:
            . . . now begin this work of pain [pp. 1–2],

and rarely changes this note throughout.

Each book contains one great misfortune for Mano. The first has his rejected love, the second the murder of his sister, the third book has his banishment and the fourth his death. But a considerable part of the first book is devoted to the story of Riculf, a robber chief whom Mano destroys, and in the second book there are accounts of the Norman wars in Italy, of the heretic Vilgardus Grammaticus and of a vision of Hell. Only in the third and fourth books does the subsidiary matter drop away to leave clearly in view the story of Mano and his adverse fate. This construction achieves interesting complexity at the beginning of the story and intensity at its ending.

Dixon's medieval world is that of the chronicles rather than the romances. He gives lively portraits of the men of the age, pictures of social misery, of ferocious asceticism and all the manifestations of the tenth century's mixture of piety and savagery; but, more than this, his very ideas are medieval, so that the fatalistic cast of thought and all the philosophical asides of Fergant contribute as much to the single consistent atmosphere of the poem as his comments on the different tactics in battle of medieval Ungrians and Normans do. The fantastic elements in *Mano* do not dispel this atmosphere. Demons frighten Norman horses in the Alps and assist the Saracens in battle, two of the poem's chief characters are fiends (the 'valley-wight' of the Riculf episode and the woman who seduces Mano in Book II) but the magic is the kind of magic found in those chronicles which portray Gerbert as a sorcerer and tell of the evil omens that filled the last years of the tenth century. There is no sophistication in Dixon's treatment of necromancy and the supernatural, no suggestion of a nineteenth-century observer looking back condescendingly to barbarous and distant superstitions, for Dixon has submerged himself completely in the personality of his invented medieval narrator. The success of *Mano* stems from this self-identification.

Fergant, like the Monk of Osneyford in 'Love's Consolation', is a gentle, contemplative, humane and sadly-wise ascetic. Once a disciple of Gerbert, he is set by him to guide and wait upon Mano and to make reports upon his behaviour, but he grows to love the knight more than he does his old master and therefore loyally accompanies Mano even after his banishment. Through Fergant Dixon does in *Mano* what he had set out to do in the *Church History*, that is adopt the point of view of 'a fair minded contemporary', and in adopting a narrator of this kind Dixon forgoes the story-teller's right of entry into the inner lives of his characters. He rests content with the merely lifelike viewpoint from which one may hear the words and see the actions of other people but can do no more than conjecture their thoughts and motives.

Thus we see no farther into the poem's hero than a closely observant and charitable friend might see, and Mano's character retains to the end a certain element of mystery. He is in many respects a perfect knight,

> He is a knight of courage high and haught,
> But mild and courteous, just and temperate [p. 58],

and his magnanimity and loyalty are contrasted with Gerbert's regard for statecraft above friendship. His temperamental fault is a proud recklessness which in the strict sense is a fatal flaw, since it betrays him into the 'dark intricate coils' of his evil destiny. As his own epitaph he writes

> I, who to Destiny was ever thrall,
> End by her deed my course by her begun:
> And honours and desire of life let fall. [p. 186]

Perhaps he is so completely the toy of Fate and accident that he is not truly a tragic hero, but he induces in us

72

something akin to tragic emotions by his steadfastness against the irresistible forces which overwhelm him.

Early in the poem Mano fancifully links Gerbert with Fortune:

> that man to me hath shown
> The thirling point of Fortune's fatal spear
> And by her hand upon it lays his own. [p. 54]

In the event this is more than merely fanciful, for Gerbert acts as an instrument of Fate when he sacrifices the knight's happiness and safety for the sake of his own policies. Gerbert overshadows and influences Mano in the poem much as in historical fact he overshadowed and influenced his contemporaries. Dixon had written in his Arnold Prize Essay:

> The many sided intellectual activity of this man; his immense engagements in the business of the world; his vastly extensive genius which fed upon everything; his tumultuary passions; have invested his name with a grandeur and mystery truly medieval. Men said that he was a magician. . . . Thus only could they account for his rise from a poor and obscure position to the highest place in Christendom: for his ubiquity, the lion-like and restless spirit with which he roamed over Italy, France, and Spain, filling all Europe with his presence; for the amazing disdain with which he received his honours; for the energy which burst forth from him as a consuming fire upon all opposition.

In *Mano* the comprehensive mind of Gerbert is well displayed, and whenever he appears he brings glimpses of the larger world that lies outside the vision of Mano and Joanna. His dealings with these two are cynically selfish throughout, although never maliciously hostile.

The other characters who work against Mano are more slightly sketched, but do not lack individuality. The woman-fiend of Book II is a compelling figure who oddly combines the mundane vitality of Ariosto's witches and Amazons with the decadent romantic strangeness of a 'femme fatale'. She enters the story to deal one savage blow against Mano and leaves as abruptly as she came. Diantha's villainy is more mischievous and less calculating. The

murderous, sordid Robert is a thoroughgoing scoundrel, but
he is less afflicting than his Fool, whose presence in the prison
and ride on an ass beside the execution cart add a touch of
bizarre horror to Mano's death. Other members of Dixon's
portrait gallery of vicious characters are well diversified in a
range extending from the crude Riculf and Elfeg (Diantha's
lover), through the unjust judge of Laurentius's children, to
the subtle and shadowy 'valley-wight'.

Pictures of virtue are fewer. There are slight sketches of
true knights in Mannus (Mano's foster-father), Giroie
(Blanche's husband) and Duke Richard of Normandy,
whose historical character is whitewashed by Dixon, and
there are more fully drawn pictures of beautiful, innocent
and courageous women in Joanna, Blanche and Laurentius's
daughter Constance.

Absence of obvious allegory and an apparent lack of
moral judgments made it difficult for its first readers to find
an underlying *motif* in *Mano*. Coventry Patmore, the reviewers and even the sympathetic Hopkins were baffled,
and Dixon had to explain to Hopkins—'so far as I can judge
myself, there should be a central motive in faith (in its
human aspect fidelity) struggling with fate or accident and
misunderstanding'.[1] Hopkins, Patmore and the others must
have been looking for something other than this—an explicit 'message' for the nineteenth century perhaps—for
they could hardly have overlooked the frequently obtruded
theme of man's predicament among the 'dark intricate toils
of Fate'.

Fate, fortune and destiny are referred to with increasing
frequency as the story unfolds. Fate is most often described
metaphorically as a wind that drives a man whither it will
and may overset him, or as a trap; but towards the end it is
once imagined as a grim beast approaching its selected
victim, so that at this point we almost lose sight of the
inscrutability and aloofness of Fate which Dixon elsewhere
indicates:

---

[1] *Correspondence*, pp. 117–18.

Dark-working Fate, who turnest with thy hand
The spherèd stars that measure human days,
How may we know thy work, or understand
(As He who set thee on the cosmic ways)
The lot that thou dost portion out to each,
The lines that thou dost spin in thy dark maze?
[pp. 167, 168]

It is apparent from this passage that Dixon utilizes the medieval conception of Fate as the agent of God. Fortune, too, is conceived medievally:

fortune, which by God's decree
Within the sweep of Fate's all-dragging powers
Reserves in earth's events contingency,
And this or that, with heart prudential
Against the set of things drives diversely. [p. 96]

This notion of Fortune as made up of the seemingly contradictory earthly manifestations of Destiny, which, in turn, is the 'minister general' of Divine Providence, was defined in the Middle Ages from Boethius, whose writings were, of course, well known to the historical Gerbert and so serve appropriately as the basis of Fergant's philosophy. Mano's changing fortunes make up a tragedy of determinism in which Fate marks down its victim and uses the instruments of human character and seemingly blind accident to destroy him.

Destiny, according to medieval doctrine, is only the executant of a higher law. So, in *Mano*, beyond the seeming capriciousness of malicious Fate is the reason and law of God:

But speak no more of fate and fatal wound:
Say rather that transgression pays the price. [p. 120]

Thus Mano's misfortunes are explicable as the punishment for his allowing himself to be seduced by the woman-fiend whom he met in the Alps. However, Dixon's poem is concerned primarily not with the justness of the hand that directs Fate but with the terrestrial outcome, in terms of human hopes and miseries, of Fate's workings. There is an incongruity between the intellectual and correctly religious attitude to Fate implied in the passages just quoted and in the poem's last lines,

> The mighty workers of this world's affairs,
> Fatality, infinity, these two,
> The one the only yoke the other wears [p. 192]

and the emotional attitude which is implicit in the whole fearful, doubt-filled atmosphere of *Mano*. More emphasis is placed upon pity and charity than upon justice. *Mano*'s essence is, as Hopkins observed, 'humanity', and Dixon's own humane nature speaks through Fergant's wide compassion, occasionally in phrases that are peculiarly Dixonian:

> Betwixt or vice or virtue ye who live
> The trembling balanced life, both pure and frail,
> Will ye not to that man some pity give
> Whomever dark temptations do assail?
> Or doth the leaf still hanging on the bough
> Laugh at his brother driven down the gale? [p. 80]

Dixon invites our pity especially for pathetic lovers who are ridden by ungovernable passions. His attitude to human love is revealed in the title of the canto 'Of the Crosses of Love', and in the words with which he describes the birth of Mano's love for Blanche:

> it did befall
> That Mano cast his eyes on Blanche the Fair:
> And of a bitter love became the thrall. [p. 17]

Mano's first loves, the melancholy pining for Blanche and the degrading infatuation with the Alpine fiend, bring him nothing but distress. His third love, comprehended on the journey back from Rome, confessed under the shadow of death and consummated only in a kiss upon the point of death, serves merely to offer him a cruelly brief glimpse of happiness the enjoyment of which will be straightway prevented. In *Mano*, as in *Love's Consolation, Concealment* and *Perversity*, Dixon's conception of human love admits little more than its painful and enigmatic aspects.

Frustrated passion and world-weariness, so prominent in
Mano, are of course common themes in Pre-Raphaelite art;
and Dixon's unhappy, frustrated Joanna has all the features
of the Pre-Raphaelite heroine:

> Her day of fairest beauty seemed to rise,
>> When sorrow and long love had made her brow
> Tenderly radiant, as the hanging skies
> When the south wind moves every wingèd bough:

>> one lovely fold,
> That seemed to gather to grave thought her eyes,
>> Of bygone sorrow and old anguish told,

> Light as a bird she seemed in these dark holds
> Of sin and woe, soft-footed as a dove:
> No fairer soul the Mother's glance beholds,
>> Since that she joined the virgin choir above,
> And woe is ceased with her, and tears and sighs,
> Which was the most she gained of earthly love.
>> [pp. 174, 175, 23]

She is the subject of several portraits in a poem full of word
painting. Among the many word pictures the vision of Hell
in Book II, Canto XII, which Patmore admired greatly, and
the description of the lark's flight that opens Canto XVII
of Book I are especially memorable. But the excellence of
the poem does not lie in such isolated passages. Short
quotations do Dixon little justice, for *Mano*'s chief appeal
lies in the cumulative effect of the whole.

The metre, a strong, disciplinary, unobtrusive *terza rima*,
makes for levelness, and under Dixon's hand it forms an
admirable vehicle for unhurrying but never slackening
narrative. Saintsbury, although he thought *Mano*'s verse
form not properly Dantesque and lacking the inevitable-
ness of all great metres, allowed it to be 'the capital and,
probably for a long, if not all time, the standard example
of English *terza rima*'.[1] Swinburne wrote to Dixon

you have put more life and spirit into the form of verse, given

---

[1] *History of English Prosody*, 1923, iii. 361.

it more straightforwardness and ease, than any other poet who
has tried it in English: and as I have just been re-reading Dante,
it is perhaps a greater tribute to your triumphant success than it
would otherwise have been to say how greatly I am struck by the
wonderful power and grace with which you have adapted this
metre to original narrative in a language so different from his.

The language of *Mano* has an archaic flavour which only
rarely makes for obscurity. Dixon's friends were not happy
about it; Hopkins asked for a 'Dixonary' and Bridges
suggested that later editions 'for use in schools' would need
to have a glossary. But I do not think that archaisms
impede our enjoyment of the poem. There are fewer than
fifty strange words, including both archaisms and 'learned',
anglicized Latin words, and we have no difficulty in immediately understanding them. The peculiarities of diction are
justified in their effect. They never strike us as an intrusive
trick, but seem to be an organic part of Fergant's appropriate idiom and of the 'furnishings' of the story. So they
contribute to that consistency of atmosphere which is the
poem's great merit.

The reviewers were a little perplexed by *Mano*. Lang
wrote cautiously: 'We have read Canon Dixon's poem, if
not constantly with ease, yet often with pleasure, and
always with sympathy and respect for work so well wrought
and original.'[1] Hall Caine proclaimed that it was 'in many
respects an important work, and in some ways the most
remarkable poetic product of the time',[2] but he was unable
to come to grips with it and spent much of his review trying,
with little success, to determine the category of poetry into
which it should fall. But Dixon's poem cannot be cate-
gorized; it differs from all the other narrative poems on
medieval legend and history that proliferated in Victoria's
reign. Few of those poems create an atmosphere with the
consistency of *Mano*, and a few have *Mano*'s emotional
intensity. Dixon does not, like Tennyson, view his subject in
the light of Victorian moral standards; he is not so plainly

[1] *Saturday Review*, 8 September 1883, p. 314.
[2] *Academy*, 1 September 1883, p. 137.

egotistical as most romantic poets; while, for all his lack of introspection, his poem has more feeling and is more moving than those objective, intellectually and emotionally shallow long poems which Morris wrote in the 1860s and later. *Mano* stands apart too from Dixon's other work. Nothing in the shorter narratives on classical or medieval subjects (except the monkish narrator of 'Love's Consolation') hints at anything found in *Mano*. Dixon's poetic impulse worked fitfully, and was sometimes not even strong enough to carry a short lyric through to a successful conclusion. Yet *Mano*, surprisingly, is a triumph of organization, discipline and poetic stamina.

Mano has depth. Dixon not only paints for us a consistent imaginative picture of a past age which he saw plain and whole, but also, by making his central motive the vain struggle of human faith against 'fate or accident and misunderstanding' and playing down the Christian interpretation of Fate, and by setting this struggle in an anarchical, doubt-ridden world, he movingly comments on the predicament of modern man, whom he sees as the bewildered victim of circumstances, hurled to and fro by fortune in a decaying and disintegrating society. *Mano* has the form, the 'architecture', that a long poem should have. Dixon is in full control of his material and nothing in the poem is out of place. His complex world of people, ideas and events, informed at all levels by his scholarship and his humanity, possesses that independent life that we expect to find in significant works of art. *Mano* is well wrought as an imaginative whole; it achieves the cumulative effect proper to a long poem. Goethe declared: 'Beware of attempting a large work. . . . What exertion and expenditure of mental force are required to arrange and round off a great whole; and then what powers, and what a tranquil, undisturbed situation in life, to express it with the proper fluency!'[1] In view of the conditions under which his poem was written, Dixon's success is surprising. *Mano* is comparable with the heroic achievement of the *Church History*.

[1] Quoted by W. M. Dixon in *English Epic and Heroic Poetry*, 1912, p. 326.

Shortly after *Mano*'s publication Dixon's work in the diocese of Carlisle was rewarded in some measure when the Bishop, Harvey Goodwin, presented him to the living of Warkworth in Northumberland. Warkworth was one of the richest livings in the Bishop's gift, but Dixon would have been better suited had Goodwin appointed him, as he could have done, to a residential canonry at Carlisle, and so afforded him better facilities for his work on the *Church History*. Intellectually Dixon was head and shoulders above most of the northern parish clergy, and so his friends were angered by the Church's failure to find him a place commensurate with his learning, while he too felt the injustice and recognized the emptiness of the one reward he had received—an honorary canonry. In his last year at Hayton he composed an epigram against his Bishop:

> Munere me duplici jucundus episcopus auxit:
> Sumque decanus inops et sine dote canon,[1]

which he wrote in the Service Book but blotted out before he left the parish. Towards the end of 1883 he made his last entry in the Service Book, a 'Valediction to Cumberland' in Latin elegiacs, gave a small present to every child in the village and left for his new parish. He was inducted in Warkworth Church on 30 November 1883.

[1] H. C. Beeching printed this epigram in 'Pages from a Private Diary', *Cornhill Magazine*, March 1898, p. 390, and added his own 'doggerel' translation:

> My lord, to show his favour
> For my good service here,
> Has given me double labour
> And halved my provender.

5

Warkworth and the
Daniel Press Publications

Dixon's new home, like the one he had left, was set in lovely countryside where there was much to delight an antiquary, while Warkworth village itself was far more attractive than Hayton. It was dominated by the Percies' great ruined castle, from which the main street, lined with substantial stone houses, ran steeply down to a Norman church and an eighteenth-century vicarage, with the tree-shaded River Coquet sweeping round close beside them, to flow under an old bridge with a guard tower at one end, and on into the North Sea a mile or so away. A short distance up river was the medieval hermitage, cut into the rock cliff, where Bishop Percy lodged his famous Hermit. Dixon's study in the vicarage overlooking the river was a large, dingy, untidy room full of stray papers and books piled haphazardly upon tables and chairs, so that his visitors often had difficulty in knowing where to sit down. Visitors came more frequently than to Hayton. 'There I visited him many times,' recalled Bridges, 'and have spent so many days that the dilapidated armchair under Severn's little drawing of Keats by the study fire seemed to belong to me.'[1] Neighbours were more interesting too. Mandell Creighton was vicar of

---

[1] *Selected Poems*, p. xl. The Severn drawing was reproduced in *Odes, Sonnets and Lyrics of John Keats*, Daniel Press, 1895.

Embleton near by, and their common interest in ecclesiastical history brought him and Dixon into close friendship.
As at Hayton Dixon was well loved, though not fully
understood, by his parishioners. He worked hard, especially
in his first three years when he was without a curate.
Travelling in all kinds of weather to make visits and conduct
the 'cottage services' which he instituted in distant parts of
the parish further impaired his fragile health, while his new
Bishop soon became aware of his capabilities and began to
load him with extra duties which he undertook without
complaint and the Bishop profited by without acknowledgment.

Before leaving Hayton Dixon had begun to prepare for
publication a small verse collection of three odes and three
eclogues. Bridges had arranged for it to be printed in
Oxford on Henry Daniel's private press, and it was issued—
a handsome slim volume called *Odes and Eclogues*—early in
1884 in an edition of a hundred copies. In the eclogues
Dixon returned to a form which he had used somewhat
unprofitably in 'Orpheus' and 'The Birth of Apollo' in
Historical Odes. Those early eclogues had not closely followed Greek or Latin models, for their mythological subjects were plastered with over-elaborate detail and shrouded
in an aura of transcendental philosophizing. The eclogues of
the 1884 volume are, by contrast, simple narratives. They
are marked by a formality and restraint that Dixon had
probably learned from Bridges, for we know that all three
were written after 1880.

Dixon's individual sensibility is more obvious in the odes,
notably in 'The Fall of the Leaf', where he realizes vividly
and lovingly the outward appearance of natural objects and,
in projecting his feelings into them, seems to endow them
with mysterious life:

> Rise in their place the woods: the trees have cast,
> Like earth to earth, their children: now they stand
> Above the graves where lie their very last:
> Each pointing with her empty hand
> And mourning o'er the russet floor,

Naked and dispossessed:
The queenly sycamore,
The linden, and the aspen, and the rest.

But thou, fair birch, doubtful to laugh or weep,
Who timorously doth keep
From the sad fallen ring thy face away;
Would'st thou look to the heavens which wander grey,
The unstilled clouds, slow mounting on their way?
They not regard thee, neither do they send
One breath to wake thy sighs, nor gently tend
Thy sorrow or thy smile to passion's end.

Lo, there on high the unlighted moon is hung,
A cloud among the clouds: she giveth pledge,
Which none from hope debars,
Of hours that shall the naked boughs re-fledge
In seasons high: her drifted train among
Musing she leads the silent song,
Grave mistress of white clouds, as lucid queen of stars.

'Ode on Conflicting Claims' explores a conflict between the
duty of relieving social misery and the impulse towards an
'aesthetic withdrawal' into the pleasures of the imagination.
This passage reveals its strength and weakness:

Thou thinkest that if none in all the rout
Who compass thee about
Turn full their soul to that which thou desirest,
Nor seek to gain thy goal,
Beauty, the heart of beauty,
The sweetness, yea, the thoughtful sweetness,
The one right way in each, the best,
Which satisfies the soul,
The firmness lost in softness, the touch of typical meetness,
Which lets the soul have rest;
Those things to which thyself aspirest:—
That they, though born to quaff the bowl divine,
As thou art, yield to the strict law of duty;
And thou from them must thine example take,
Leave the amaranthine vine,
And the prized joy forsake.

Supple, excited verse and direct language convey Dixon's thought and feeling until, it seems, his own linguistic resources fail and he totters lamely into that devalued, inflated, 'poetic' diction of 'quaff the bowl divine'.

All three odes are full of that tender sympathy and melancholy resignation in which Dixon's most characteristic work is conceived; while both odes and eclogues have the virtues of grace and economy which had been lacking in most of Dixon's earlier work. The reviewers were kind and noted with approval the poet's qualities of sympathy and reserve, but by the manner of its publication *Odes and Eclogues* could not be expected to claim much attention. So it cannot be supposed that Dixon's reputation was great enough to give him much hope when he came forward in November 1885 as a candidate for the Chair of Poetry at Oxford. On 11 November *The Oxford Magazine* published a note advocating his claims, but a fortnight later, the day before the election, it was announced that he had withdrawn his name. Then, in what was described as an 'animated' election, Palgrave, as befitted the man who had the blessing of both Matthew Arnold and the Poet Laureate, defeated his remaining rival Courthope.

Dixon returned to the *Church History* and began to write the fourth volume cheered by appreciative reviews of the third; but the work went slowly, for he was aging and tired and had undertaken other labours. Having become rural dean in succession to his friend Creighton who had been appointed Dixie Professor of Ecclesiastical History at Cambridge, he found diocesan work crowding in upon him just as it had done at Hayton. There was more work for his pen, too, as he contributed the first of several articles to the recently founded *English Historical Review* and to the *Dictionary of National Biography*, then in its second year of majestic progress. Most of his dozen contributions to *D.N.B.* were upon the men of the English Reformation, but he wrote also on John Dobson, the architect of Newcastle, and on some Methodists, including his father and a Mrs. Agnes Bulmer who was the author of 'probably the longest work in verse ever composed by a woman'. Furthermore Dixon was busy editing for Routledge a *Bible Birthday Book* and was revising poems for his second Daniel Press volume, to be called *Lyrical Poems*. As was his custom he sent his poems to Bridges and Hopkins and accepted some of the emendations which they proposed.

At the beginning of June 1886 he was in London for the Colonial Exhibition and the Royal Academy Summer Exhibition, but liked neither. From London he went on to stay with Bridges at Yattendon, where he heard with satisfaction of the defeat of Gladstone's iniquitous Irish Home Rule Bill and the split in the Liberal Party. He returned to Warkworth in July, mentioned the General Election, which was then proceeding, in a sermon on the text 'All flesh is grass', and was gratified by the Conservative and Unionists' success. He plunged with renewed vitality into parochial work and established another 'cottage service' in an outlying hamlet. There were now four cottage services, three established since his arrival, and he was still without a curate.

Lyrical Poems was published in an edition of a hundred and five copies at the beginning of 1887. On 1 February Bridges wrote to Henry Daniel:

> Yr vol. of Dixon's poems just arrived. If ambition still lurks in your noble mind you must be grateful to me for my introduction. Your press will hereafter be very famous. The editio princeps of these masterpieces—for some of them, (most of them), are such—will be a prize indeed. They have an imaginative quality which has been given in this world only to some dozen poets if as many, & Dixon's lyrics will go with the best in English—Shelley, Shakespeare & Blake.

Saintsbury also compared Dixon's 'poetry in the matrix' with Blake's for 'astonishing poetic quality' and 'want of finish'.[1] Such a comparison is not extravagant, for there is an imaginative penetration, a limpidity and freshness comparable with Blake's in some of the songs in this volume. In them, although Nature's aspects are described in terms of

---

[1] *History of English Prosody*, iii. 359.

human emotion and activity, Dixon does not seem to project his own feelings into the natural scene but rather to look upon an objective reality unaffectedly. In 'Sky that rollest ever' we have the illusion that the relationship between sky and river exists somehow outside any human observation of it:

> Sky, that rollest ever,
>   It is given to thee
> To roll above the river
>   Rolling to the sea.
>
> Truer is thy mirror
>   In the lake or sea;
> But thou lovest error
>   More than constancy.
>
> And the river running
>   Fast into the sea,
> His wild hurry shunning
>   All thy love and thee;
>
> Not a moment staying
>   To return thy smiles,
> Sees thee still displaying
>   All thy sunny wiles:
>
> Till thou fallest weeping:
>   Then more furiously
> All his wild waves leaping
>   Rush into the sea.

A comparable effect is created in another Song:

> Oh, what shall lift the night,
>   The lightning or the moon?
> There is no other light,
>   The day is gone too soon.
>
> The lightning with his flash
>   An instant and no more,
> Is as an angel's lash
>   Smiting the dusk-loved shore.

> The moon with trembling light
> From her pale shell of sleep
> Shall kindlier break the night
> Of yon thick clouds that weep.

The ode 'The Spirit Wooed' is equally direct and unaffected. It is an invocation to the 'Spirit of the Sphere', the essence of beauty, harmony and joy; it is also an admirable 'evening piece' full of happy descriptive touches:

> Art thou gone so far,
> Beyond the poplar tops, beyond the sunset-bar,
> Beyond the purple cloud that swells on high
> In the tender fields of sky? . . .
> O come thou again!
> Be seen on the falling slope: let thy footsteps pass
> Where the river cuts with his blue scythe the grass:
> Be heard in the voice that across the river comes
> From the distant wood, even when the stilly rain
> Is made to cease by light winds: come again,
> As out of yon grey glooms,
> When the cloud grows luminous and shiftily riven,
> Forth comes the moon, the sweet surprise of heaven:
> And her footfall light
> Drops on the multiplied wave: her face is seen
> In evening's pallor green:
> And she waxes bright
> With the death of the tinted air: yea, brighter grows
> In sunset's gradual close.

Hopkins wrote in a letter,

'The Spirit Wooed' is a lovely piece of nature and imagination all in one, in a vein peculiarly yours: I do not believe there is anyone that has so much of Wordsworth's insight into nature as you have. Then it seems to me the *temper* is exactly right, a thing most rare, which of Tennyson and Browning and most of our modern poets can by no means be said. . . .

The directness of *the Spirit Wooed* distinguishes it and other of your poems from Wordsworth's in the same kind: his are works of reflection, they are self-conscious, and less spontaneous, but then the philosophy in them explains itself the clearer on that account.[1]

Certainly Dixon's poem has no palpable designs upon us. We are aware simply of an acute, tremblingly alive sensibility enjoying a private vision. Only in the concluding section does Dixon turn towards the reader and make his generalized statement of a personal sense of loneliness, deprivation, and, in the last words, despair:

> Can the weeping eye
> Always feel light through mists that never dry?
> Can empty arms alone for ever fill
> Enough the breast? Can echo answer still,
> When the voice has ceased to cry?

Bridges called the other ode in this volume—'On Advancing Age'—'one of the most fearfully sad things ever written'. In it Dixon announces the dominant theme of *Lyrical Poems*—mutability. External nature mirrors man's moods, and the empty shore, the restless sea and the melancholy cries of the birds reflect man's awareness of the frailty and solitariness of old age and his fear of the wide emptiness of death:

> Thou goest more and more
> To the silent things: thy hair is hoar,
> Emptier thy weary face: like to the shore
> Far-ruined, and the desolate billow white,
> That recedes and leaves it waif-wrinkled,
>   gap-rocked, weak . . .
>
> The breakers dash, the smitten spray drops
>   to the roar;
> The spit upsprings, and drops again,
> Where'er the white waves clash in the main.
> Their sound is but one: 'tis the cry
> That has risen from of old to the sky,
> 'Tis their silence!

[1] *Correspondence*, pp. 55–6, 57.

Go now from the shore
Far-ruined: the grey shingly floor
To the crashing step answers; the doteril cries,
And on dipping wing flies:
'Tis their silence!
And thou, oh thou
To that wild silence sinkest now.
No more remains to thee than the cry of silence,
the cry
Of the waves, of the shore, of the bird to the sky.

Dixon simultaneously catches the very atmosphere of the scene and communicates a personal predicament. By contrast he adopts an entirely objective method in the Song 'Why fadest thou in death?' where he evokes a mood merely by the terms in which he describes an autumnal scene:

Why fadest thou in death,
Oh yellow waning tree?
Gentle is autumn's breath,
And green the oak by thee.

But with each wind that sighs
The leaves from thee take wing;
And bare thy branches rise
Above their drifted ring.

'Nature and Man' sets the seasonal renewal of nature's beauties beside the aging of the individual human being:

To mock us thus with change,
From fair to fair to range,
Dissolving thy most fair
Into a change as rare,
Leaving our hearts behind,
Oh, Nature, art thou kind? . . .

With laughter thou dost greet
The human sigh and groan
That mourns the thing that's gone.
Thou laughest, for thy store
Holds beauty evermore . . .

Then thou thyself dost tire
Of the unfilled desire
With which we thee pursue:
Therefore, with sudden view
Thou shewest us a glass
To see ourselves—Alas,
Grey we are grown, and old:
Our fancied heat is cold,
Our shaking limbs are dry:
We see ourselves, and die.

In 'A Country Place Revisited' the return to an old haunt after long absence provokes similar thoughts:

My foot returns: the same wild tree
Waves in the hedgerow over me.
I knew not then, I know not now
The leaves that hang upon her bough.
But I recall her wind-vexed form
Tossed in a sort of mimic storm,
And threatening all those leaves to cast
If wilder grew the sportive blast.
And how the bold and merry wind
Grew silent suddenly, I mind:
The wind, that summer's sweets had made
More bold to dare the silvan maid.
    The summer breeze still plays as free,
And shakes the ringlets of the tree:
But I, who watched them then as now,
Turn I to them as calm a brow;
Or can I smile to see their play
As blithe as on the former day?
Thought, that comes first as fantasy,
Sadly returns as memory.
She looks with question from the eyes
Whence first she laughed with glad surprise:
And thence descending to the heart
Ends with a sigh her former part;
Filling the sketch that first she drew
With graver touch than then she knew.

Here thought and feeling are sharply focused in a single intense experience. Such a focus is lacking in 'Nature and

Man' which makes, by contrast, a blurred impression upon the reader.

Many of the other poems in this volume are more seriously blurred. These include 'Both Less and More', a snatch of dreamlike narrative in which the details of a mystery are lightly sketched, two poems prompted by scientific advances—'Vain Ambition', which ponders dismally upon the vastness of stellar distances, and the Darwinian 'Man's Coming'—the unchristian 'Life and Death', and 'Unrest' which faces despairingly the fact of life's shortness and, like 'Ode on Advancing Age', offers no hope of an after life.

In *Lyrical Poems*, especially in the two odes, the songs and 'A Country Place Revisited', Dixon works more assuredly within his own true but narrow range than he had done in *Christ's Company* or *Historical Odes*, and with unstudied fastidiousness chooses his impressions of objects to convey his feelings of pity and sorrow as he looks upon a world of change and dissolution. The reviewers noted this fastidiousness, this delicacy of imagination. Beeching in the *Academy* was unrestrained in his admiration and quoted all 'The Spirit Wooed', exclaiming that it 'takes rank with the finest in English'.[1] Other reviewers found some things to dispraise, but approved the sweetness and tunefulness of the shorter lyrics.

The appearance of *Lyrical Poems* coincided with a return of Dixon's ill health. He fell sick on a visit to London in January 1887 and was laid up there for several days. In May he wrote to Bridges from Warkworth

I have not been doing much: least of all in poetry. I am slowly forging ahead with my 4th volume of history: but find the work heavy & less satisfactory. This once new year has indeed brought me little but trouble as yet. Everything goes wrong in the parish; I am misrepresented &c., and there are rows of all sorts: school rows, master & mistress leaving: young men's club rows, &c.—but I will not bore you.

'Curate is gone to the east' (Isn't there something like that in Tennyson?) Yes, he went off ill with a Cook's tour, & is I fear

[1] 18 June 1887, p. 428.

like to come back this month ill again with coast fever. Meanwhile I have a deputy curate, as old as myself, but as strong as a lion, who does pretty well. He is from the south, Cornwall, rather an odd fellow: very high: what one might call a mass priest. He does all kind of things in celebrating: but tolerates my simplicity. . . .

Daniel is considering whether he will publish that story of Theodosius & Eudocia which I sent you along with the Preface of which you saw a draft. I now call it the Story of Eudocia & her Brothers. There is a 2nd part of it wh. no one has seen: that may perhaps follow: but will want great trouble taken with it. . . .

My aged friend the curate pro temp. is sitting with his back to me, reading. Enormous back! enormous legs! vast connecting part! He has made nothing of life, but is as happy as a king, enters into converse with the people here, and knows more of them and does them more good than I do. Preaches as if he were the pope: and many ladies, who care not if I died tomorrow, come after him, & congratulate him on his sermon, and sun themselves before him.

Bridges did not entertain a high opinion of Dixon's new poem, but Daniel approved of it: 'not so much as a poem as because I consider it a most happy study of Byzantine life and character'.[1] So *The Story of Eudocia and her Brothers* was issued from the Daniel Press in March 1888 in an edition of fifty copies.

Eudocia is a narrative in heroic couplets, about 750 verses long, with a Preface on the use of the couplet. We may leave Daniel to be the judge of its historical felicity but we can agree that its poetic merit is secondary, for here, more than anywhere else in his verse, Dixon's imagination is 'deadened by historical predilection'.[2] The story of the humble Eudocia's marriage to the Emperor Theodosius and their misunderstanding over an apple contained the material for high

[1] Letter to Rees (Bodley MS.,Don.e.20, fol. 36).

[2] *Selected Poems*, p. xxxviii. Dixon told Daniel that his historical sources were Gibbon and Finlay. Finlay writes 'The eventful life of Eudocia, the wife of Theodosius II, does not require to borrow romantic incidents from Eastern tales; it only asks for genius in the narrator to unfold a rich web of romance.'

melodrama, as Massinger's *The Emperor of the East* had shown, but Dixon under-emphasizes the passionate element in his story and fails to realize its drama. There is little attempt at incisive characterization and the language suffers from what can be described as anaemia—a meagreness in connotation and a lack of vitality, colour and concentration. The reviewers slashed the poem. The *Athenaeum* declared 'Canon Dixon tells the story of Eudocia . . . in what he considers narrative poetry in the couplet verse used by Chaucer', quoted the poem's bald opening lines, and added 'There are nearly a thousand lines of this.'[1] Bridges wrote to Dixon on 16 August 1888

A Londoner was down here & brought his Atheneum down with him. He was reading it in my garden on Sunday aftn. I said I wonder you waste your time reading that dullest of dull journals. He said I always read it, it tells one what's going on.— Does it? said I—He, to justify himself thought to entertain me & began reading to me from it the opening of Eudocia—Is not that about the worst verse you ever heard? he asked—& who is Canon Dixon?—Does not the Atheneum tell you?—No—'He's a great friend of mine; I cannot defend his Eudocia, but the reviewer is a muff if he treats it as the work of a 2nd rate man.' So I fetched him some of your poems—& that evening we c^d not detach him from your history. He sent to Daniel for yr poems & was much disappointed to find one lot out of print. But why inflict on me the onus of explaining your authorship of Eudocia? Daniel & you aren't to be trusted. . . .

Coming so soon after the success of his other two Daniel Press books the hostile reception given to *Eudocia* was doubly mortifying to Dixon, particularly as Daniel had invited him to write more 'Byzantine sketches'. Indeed, as soon as *Eudocia* was off the press Dixon had prepared to take in hand its sequel, the story of Eudocia's daughter Eudoxia. The historical sources for Eudoxia's story would provide him with a wealth of dramatic incident and a direful background of the crumbling Western Empire in the days of Attila, but we have no means of telling how he handled

[1] 28 July 1888, p. 128.

his material, since 'Eudoxia' was never printed and is now lost. Other poems, including eclogues and songs, that Dixon was writing about this time are lost likewise.

In the two years following the publication of *Eudocia* Dixon suffered from attacks of bronchitis and pneumonia that foreshadowed a more serious breakdown in health. He was tied to labour at his *History*, and for long periods could find neither the leisure nor the will to write verse. Moreover he was greatly saddened by the deaths of two dear friends. In June 1889 a pained and angry letter from Bridges carried the news of Hopkins's death, and five months later Dixon received the equally distressing news that Edwin Hatch had died. Labouring under ill health and his burden of parochial and diocesan duties, Dixon at last managed to finish the troublesome fourth volume of his *History*. He wrote the last page in March 1890 and noted this fact in his diary with a 'Laus Deo'. The favourable reviews earlier of the third and now of the fourth volume of the *History* showed that Dixon commanded serious attention as a scholar in his field, and he was proposed for the Dixie Chair when Creighton vacated it for the Bishopric of Peterborough, 'but', says Bridges, 'after a few days' demur he determined not to stand, feeling, I think, that with his years and health he might expect an appointment free from the worry and uncertainty of competition'.[1] Owing to his breakdown in health in the following year he gained no such appointment.

Throughout 1891 periods of activity, when he took out and revised old poems and planned new verse collections, alternated with bouts of sickness, melancholia and accidie. In December he arranged for Daniel to print a collection of Eclogues, but before he could revise and send off the poems he was struck down by influenza. 'He was delirious in the fever, and as he recovered it was seen that he was somewhat altered in mind.'[2] He had an hereditary tendency towards melancholy and a long attentuating illness was sufficient to throw him into a pathological state of depression. From December to March and again from May to September he

[1] *Selected Poems*, p. xli.   [2] *Id.*, p. xli.

was away from Warkworth, ill physically and mentally. 'Through those long dreary months his mind was obsessed by religious despondency, whose melancholy convictions were probably determined by physical debility.'[1] In a letter written on 20 August 1892 from Bournemouth where he was convalescing Dixon told Daniel of some of the effects of his illness:

> You have reason to complain of me, that I have never written, nor proceeded, after making proposals for printing some poems with you, and being accepted by you. If it were an ordinary excuse which I have to offer, I should be without excuse in offering it. But the matter is, that very soon after writing to you, I was seized with a terrible attack of influenza, near the end of December last, and this had such effects on me as I dare not describe, especially in depression of spirit. I could not any longer engage myself with preparing MSS for the press, and was obliged to give up the thought. Although the Almighty has been pleased to raise me to bodily health to a certain extent, as I gratefully acknowledge, I still remain to a considerable extent in mental depression. Again and again I have thought of writing to you to apologize, but either the thought has come when I could not do so, or I have deferred it.
>
> I sincerely hope that the inconvenience to you has been less than the surprise you must have felt at my silence. But you must, in any case, kindly forgive me. I am deeply convinced of the enormous importance of religion, in comparison with the highest & noblest of human pursuits. If I write more poetry it must be religious.

We cannot know what thoughts possessed Dixon's mind in this dark period of physical and spiritual sickness, but, clearly, he undertook the same kind of agonising heart searchings that Hopkins had made in 1881. He had been torn, as Hopkins had been, between the apparently conflicting claims of art and religion, and now, it seems, had decided that the act of poetic composition, except when related to religious subjects, was bound up with a vaingloriousness incompatible with the truly religious life. Not

---

[1] *Selected Poems*, p. xlii.

only did he resolve not to write secular verse but he destroyed existing manuscript poems. Probably the last non-religious poem that he wrote was the second part of 'The Unanswered Question'[1] which he sent to Bridges on 16 November, saying 'It is unfinished: for I lost heart and the thread.'

It is in keeping with the normal irony of circumstances that soon after Dixon had abjured secular poetry he was mentioned as a candidate for the vacant Laureateship, although he was never aware of this. A gentleman walking one morning on Putney Common met Swinburne and asked him who should be the next Poet Laureate. 'They should appoint Canon Dixon', he said oracularly and hurried on.[2] When Lord Salisbury, perhaps intending that the Laureateship should be laughed out of existence, at long last made the appointment, Dixon—we are surprised to learn—was relieved. He wrote to Bridges on 1 January 1896:

As it is not you, I am glad so perfectly inoffensive a person is chosen, who has never written anything of account, I suppose. Better than some dreadful ones we could name. I am glad that someone is made, for the delay seemed a sign of the back seat that poetry was taking in the world's eye.

Who were these more dreadful ones might admit a wide solution, but their names are not beyond all conjecture. Sir Edwin Arnold and Sir Lewis Morris spring readily to mind.

Dixon attempted to hasten his recovery from depression and sickness by travelling abroad. During an eventful three weeks' tour of Ireland in September 1893, in the course of which Mrs. Dixon's gold watch was stolen, pawned and recovered by the police, he visited the Jesuit House on St. Stephen's Green where Hopkins had died, and (he wrote to Bridges),

was courteously shewn over it by one of the Fathers who knew him well. . . . He, Father Cormac, had a great opinion of Gerard,

[1] *Selected Poems*, p. xxxiv.
[2] H. C. Beeching, 'Conference on Books and Men, IX—The Tears of the Muses', in *Cornhill Magazine*, March 1900, p. 401.

without, I think, knowing of his genius. He spoke of him as a most delightful companion, & as excellent in his calling, and so on, intimating at the same time that there was something unusual about him; that he was fond of pursuing niceties to an extent that rather stood in the way of his general usefulness. As that he dwelt on the niceties of the languages, in his classical lectures, in a way that rather stopped the progress of the classes. Also he was fond of taking up unusual subjects for himself: that when he was in Wales he took up Welsh in the most extraordinary manner, pursuing it into local dialects, & becoming so skilled that Professor Rhys said he knew it as well as himself, or nearly so.

In the following year he settled down once again to work in earnest at the *History*. Though still a sick man he had attained some degree of spiritual ease. 'I cannot but testify my gratitude to Almighty God for His mercy to me in restoring to me the hope in Him, and the peace which I had lost most justly', he wrote to Bridges, and,

I am very thankful that I have a measure of restored peace of mind, attributable solely to the mercy of God. He only He can give and take away. All but His approbation and love fade & sink. I feel very grateful to you for the letters you sent me in the depth of my trouble, and the way in which you, as it were, stuck to me. The only return that I can make is to declare that GOD in Christ is the only source of life & health in the soul: and that the traditional or orthodox view of religion is the true one. . . .

I now and then write a few sentences of history: but, oh, so slowly: so much of pottering. I have also of course weekly a sermon: a great and merciful honour, in which I find great comfort sometimes. . . .

Ever Your aff.
R. W. Dixon

I have just heard of a farmer put into the chair of the Parish Council who said he would be neither partial nor impartial, but do his duty.

Through Bridges Dixon in his later years met a group of younger poets which included Binyon, Newbolt, Beeching, Mary Coleridge and Margaret Woods. Mary Coleridge, whose poems have much in common with Dixon's, visited him at Warkworth, and always praised him highly. 'I love and venerate some of his poetry more deeply than I can say', she wrote to Daniel. Henry Newbolt came to Warkworth too, and of his visit in 1895 he recalled

Dixon was a strange, lonely and picturesque figure: his face was startlingly like that of a goat, but a goat who had received a human soul and had at last become a symbol, like one of the gods of Egypt. He was a fascinating character—exquisitely humble and courteous, but profoundly learned and with a critical gift which was in itself a kind of divination. He became interested in my play *Mordred*, and his letters about it revealed to me thoughts and devices of my own of which I had known nothing until I read the play again through his eyes.[1]

In two long letters criticizing *Mordred* Dixon displays the same sort of devoted care, insight and generosity that Hopkins had bestowed upon Dixon's work.

In November 1896 a selection by Bridges from Dixon's verse was published in the *Shilling Garland* series of modern poets, edited by Binyon. For this collection, which he called *Songs and Odes*, Bridges chose poems mostly from the Daniel Press volumes and added only one unpublished poem 'Terror'—an obscure, fleeting dream of horrid decay, death and a nameless terror. The book was given slight but favourable reviews. The *Saturday Review*, for instance, praised the poems' haunting charm, and concluded: 'If Canon Dixon's poems seem at times too intangible of substance, it is not from poverty of vein, but the fastidious choice of an artist.'[2] Dixon was pleased, but his tiny volume did not gain the wide popularity that Bridges had anticipated.

During 1896 Dixon had another attack of bronchitis and was, in his own view, 'indolent'; but he pushed the *History* steadily on into the reign of Elizabeth, performed his parochial duties and sent some newly written hymns to Bridges in October. These may have been the first poems he had written since he 'lost heart and the thread' in 1892.

---

[1] *My World as in my Time*, 1932, p. 269.   [2] 19 December 1896, p. 656.

When he was ill he was oppressed, as usual, by a sense of failure. He wrote to Bridges on 1 October:

the parish work goes on, I fear with little result: at least apparent result—I sometimes feel as if it would be for the good of the place to pass into younger hands. I have been here thirteen years. One of the great defects of our Church is long incumbencies: as a rule twelve years is enough. A man has done what he can by that time. I have made little impression, I fear.

The death of Morris this month grieved him deeply. He had not seen him for some years and had disliked the political activity that Morris had seen as no more than a logical development of the Oxford Brotherhood. 'I was never so much astonished as when he turned Socialist . . . What a contrast to John Wesley's Journal. The one tried to make this earth an Earthly Paradise, the other to point men to the skies', he wrote, and—referring to a curate—'he is a Socialist, or Communist, or whatever you call him who thinks everything is bad that is done or exists . . . he has got something in his mind that I cannot understand'. But his admiration and affection for Morris as a man were as abundant as in his youth, for in his nature they were inexhaustible. When we read his accounts of his friends in the biographies of Rossetti, Hatch, Morris, Burne-Jones and James Dixon we find a generous, unstudied veneration that attracts us as much to the biographer as to his subject. Bridges writes:

His friendship was of the sort that will not see a fault in a friend. It was absolutely generous and ideal, and would admit of no abatement whatever. It was possible to inveigle him into just criticism, and intellectually he could be fair enough, but when it led to detraction, it withered away, and left his deep feeling unaffected,[1]

and, in writing of his father's powers of admiration, Dixon reveals his own:

admiration certainly carried him beyond his judgment. . . . But then moderate admiration—discreet admiration—admiration

[1] *Selected Poems*, p. xliv.

that knows the day of its death (never living very long)—is so beautiful a thing itself that it may pardon its own excess . . . it is excessive admiration that has given birth to the most perfect portraits of greatness which the world possesses. Those who admire most are found after all to be those who know best; and from them, not from colder critics, the world receives its opinion of the great.[1]

As he contributed his Oxford reminiscences to Mackail's 'Life' of Morris, memories of the golden days of the Brotherhood came thronging back. He and the surviving brothers, Price and Burne-Jones, looked back wistfully, and Burne-Jones wrote to him:

My dear Dickides . . .
what a pity that none of us can remember more—that we kept no diary—kept no letters—but how could we forsee.

I am sure you and I when we were lads never expected to live past twenty-five—if we could have guessed a little.

And then we were lazy—at least I was.

Why did you come to town and not come to see me or send for me?

Yours aff.
Ned.

Dixon had no serious illness this year. His only troubles arose from a drunken sexton and the Communist curate, 'a holy man, very self-denying & morbidly conscientious: always making a row with some one or other', who would not say the Litany or the Prayer for the Queen 'because of the Petitions for Victory over her enemies'. He was fond of this curate, however, and sorry when he left. Except for brief visits to London to pursue his historical researches and to sit on a committee for the revision of *Hymns Ancient and Modern*, he was seldom absent from his parish. Towards the end of the year Bridges persuaded Will Rothenstein to draw him for his series of 'English Portraits', but when the drawing was done Bridges did not like it. It shows Dixon's high brow, aquiline nose, full lips, wrinkled cheeks, very shaggy eyebrows, long hair and full beard, and may have

[1] *Life of James Dixon*, pp. 345, 346.

been a fair outward likeness, but it is lifeless and unsympa-
thetic and declares nothing of the nature of the sitter.[1]

His critical illness in 1892 had robbed Dixon of one
chance of preferment, but his friends were still annoyed that
scholarship and hard labour had not yet brought him his
proper reward. Beeching, writing in the *Cornhill Magazine*
in March 1898 of the unjust system of preferment in the
Church of England, referred to Dixon's case although he
did not mention Dixon's name, and Bridges wrote a strong
letter to Stubbs, the Bishop of Oxford. Nothing was done,
possibly because of a further breakdown in his health under
another attack of bronchitis. He took a long holiday and
while convalescing visited Holland, where he heard of
Burne-Jones's death. In July he wrote to Bridges:

> It is, as you say, a shock to me and a loss to the world. . . . I
> suppose that his drawings (to say nothing of his paintings) are
> the finest ever done by an English hand, and to be put among the
> first of the world, even by those of M. Angelo. . . . There are only
> two left of our Oxford set now, C. Price and myself. It is curious
> what an effect his death has on me. It is that all life appears to
> have gone out of art. All is but toys: renown and grace is dead.[2]

Dixon's life of grace without renown continued, and in 1899
he entered his twenty-fifth year of work upon the *History*.
In August Bridges was preparing his own 'New Poems' for
the press, and asked Dixon to look over 'Eclogue I' which
commemorated their first meeting at Hayton and celebrated
their friendship:

> Man hath with man on earth no holier bond
> Than that the Muse weaves with her dreamy thread.

But the bond was shortly to be broken.

By an irony not inappropriate to the author of *Mano*,
Dixon received only in the last months of his life overdue
honours for his historical work. In October 1899 he was
admitted to an Honorary Fellowship at Pembroke and in

[1] It is reproduced in *Northern Counties Magazine*, Oct. 1900.
[2] *Selected Poems*, p. xliv.

December his University conferred upon him an Honorary D.D. degree. During his last visit to Oxford Dixon could return in reminiscence to the very earliest days when he first seized his sustaining ideals of art and brotherhood, for he stayed with Gifford, his Birmingham headmaster. Gifford urged him to continue the *History* beyond the fifth volume, which had just been completed, but Dixon said that he had little hope of doing so. He was extremely frail. He returned to Warkworth, resumed his parochial rounds over wintry roads, took influenza and died about 4 a.m. on 23 January 1900, in his sixty-seventh year. He had preached his last sermon nine days earlier, and on 17 January had made the last entry in his diary—'Finished revising Chap. XXXII of my History for the press: a most severe task.'[1]

[1] Gee, Preface to Dixon's *Church History*, v. v.

6

Epilogue

The unpublished portion of Dixon's *History*, carrying the narrative up to 1570, was seen through the press by his friend Henry Gee, and was published in 1902 in two volumes. When A. F. Pollard reviewed them he claimed that Dixon's *History* was 'the most serious contribution to the ecclesiastical history of England made within the last generation', and as a parting shot against the bishops added 'Dixon's "History" is good, but it would have been much better had he received some such position in church or university as would have given adequate scope for his undoubted historical and literary gifts.'[1]

Dixon was one of the last amateur historians in the tradition of Burnet, Macaulay and Carlyle, in that he had notable accomplishments and important interests outside history. In the later nineteenth century historians of this kind were ousted by the 'professionals', usually holders of university positions. He wrote under disadvantages, for he could not apply himself continuously to his task and lived far away from good libraries. When he began to write he was little known and had no obvious credentials as an historian; his first volume was published without any introduction to explain his object; and so it is not surprising that his work won its reputation slowly. But at his death it was widely accepted as an important contribution to the

[1] *English Historical Review*, July 1902, p. 580.

understanding of its subject and period. Dixon's patient researches brought to light so much material hitherto difficult of access that he has provided an unfailing quarry of material for most of the later serious studies of its subject, as a glance through their footnotes will prove. Moreover, the *History* itself is not yet ousted as a standard work.

Dixon tells a highly complicated story at considerable length but fully masters his material and never becomes bogged down in detail. His narrative has pace and his vision is broad. He has a feeling for the 'architecture' of an historical work and sufficient mental span to comprehend the whole of the English Reformation as he passes on through the four reigns, presenting the cynical spoliation of the Church under Henry VIII and Edward VI, the dreary fanaticism of Mary and the painstaking efforts of the Elizabethan reformers to reconstruct a lasting Church of England. He wrote consciously from the standpoint of a High Anglican defending his Church against the attacks of J. A. Froude. Profoundly aware of the continuity of the Church of England, he described as 'preposterous' the notion held by some men that she was created or had her origin at the Reformation. In his eyes the Reformers simply held to the true Catholic faith which the Romanists, through ignorance or policy, perverted. His whole learned *History* constitutes a reasoned exposition of the historical basis of the Anglican *via media*, but his first aim, of course, was to state the facts fully and as fairly as possible. To Hopkins he wrote

My aim is to get the exact truth, & give that, with whatever colour. I mean, that I do not pretend to be without prepossessions & bias; if I had not those, I should not take the labour of writing at all: but I hope never to be found suppressing, telling half a story, concealing anything connected with any point at issue, or otherwise dealing dishonestly with materials. This is what I mean by historical honesty: not the having no bias or side.[1]

---

[1] *Correspondence*, p. 34.

Although he describes events which no interested English-man can speak of without prejudice and although he is emotionally stirred by these events Dixon contrives to be calm and just. Even the Smithfield bonfires do not inflame his passions or cloud his judgment, and in the recital of those scenes of cruelty he remains cool. He praises the heroism of the martyrs and writes movingly of their suffer-ings but will not be seduced from the ascertainable facts by his feelings; so he shows what is doubtful in older narratives, he limits accurately the extent of the persecution, giving the names of the martyrs and the place and date of their suffer-ings, and he partly (but only partly) exonerates the tradi-tional scapegoats, King Philip and Bishop Bonner. His very detachment annoyed some readers, but it was his fair-mindedness that those contemporaries who were most capable of judging his work singled out for praise. Creighton said

He wrote from the point of view of a fair minded contempor-ary; he looked on things as they happened, in themselves, not palliating or excusing on account of the ultimate advantages. He was in fact observing a process, & stating its steps fairly, without any view of the end which could distort the facts. His fairness in this way was very valuable. When Father Gasquet wrote on the 'Suppression of the Monasteries' from the Roman Catholic point of view, it was found that he had little to add to Dixon who had suppressed nothing.[1]

He is fair, but he does not suspend judgment on char-acters and actions. He judges the whole Reformation finally as an event sorely needed, but 'carried out on the whole by bad instruments, and attended by great calamities (*History*, i, 7). He draws lessons from history, but, as this faintly acid passage reveals, he does not believe that history demon-strates a principle of inevitability in human affairs:

It is the humble office of the historian to prepare the way for the historical philosophers and theorists (not so rare a race), whose touch makes darkness light. The historian must not desert the region of his facts: nor expatiate in the necessitarian heaven,

[1] Letter to Rees, Bodley MS.Don.e.20, fol. 34.

when the motives and characters of the men with whom he deals are sufficient to explain the events which he relates. (ii. 213.)

So he pauses in his narrative at crises to ask why events fell as they did and to speculate on whether they might have fallen very differently. At every important turning point he takes stock of the possible developments of a situation in view of the characters of the men and women involved.

Although in the latest letters to Bridges Dixon regretted having written uncharitably of 'men better than myself', his character sketches are always just and usually generous too. These observations on Cranmer, for instance, are both acute and charitable:

Cranmer had a greater capacity than either Henry or Crumwel: he had much of the dispassionate quality of the statesman; but withal an indecision and want of readiness which laid him at the mercy of inferior men, and often produced duplicity in his own conduct. He joined innocency with a disposition to deal tenderly with himself, painfulness with love of ease, the solemnity of virtue with a morbid conscience and a tremulous sensibility to every current of opinion. This large, timorous, and unwieldy nature was needful to the men of violence and craft who now held in their hands the destinies of the country and the Church. . . .

Both his fall [the recantation] and the astonishing inspiration by which he, at least in part, retrieved it, could only have occurred in a character of many sides with an essential simplicity. He was guileless in the one and in the other: and the quality of mind that made him fall made him rise again. To think that he acted with calculation is to misunderstand him. He could calculate for others, but not for himself. . . .

His merits and services were greater than his faults. He had gravity, gentleness and innocency: boundless industry and carefulness: considerable power of forecast: and he lived in a high region. He preserved the continuity of the Church of England. He gave to the English Reformation largeness and capacity. In the weakness which he himself admitted he was servile to many influences: he turned himself many ways in the waters, and allowed himself to be carried very far: but this was not altogether to the hurt of posterity. He was a greater man than any

106

of his contemporaries. His death completed the circle of five men of episcopal degree, who loosed the yoke of Rome from the neck of the Church of England by the sacrifice of their lives: a glorious crown of bishops, the like of which is set upon the brow of no other church in Christendom. (i. 155, iv. 550, 552.)

For Dixon, as for so many other Anglicans, Cranmer's Prayer Book is the Church's most precious possession, and if the *History* may be said to have a hero, that hero is Cranmer. His stature has grown considerably over the past seventy years and Dixon's sympathetic appraisal has helped that growth. The other character studies in Dixon's *History* range from thumbnail sketches of Henry's monastic visitors to full-length portraits of Henry himself (in deliberate contrast to Froude's panegyric), Queen Mary, Latimer, Ridley, Gardiner, Bonner, Hooper, Pole, Parker and the other leading persons in his story, but all are alike vivid and vital.

Eileen Power once said 'There was once a historian who was so dull that even the other historians began to notice it.' Dixon carries his learning lightly and is never dull. He has an historical imagination that enables him to project himself into the scenes and events of the past and capture their life for his readers. Not only does he bring to life the most obviously dramatic episodes in his story, such as the trials of the heretics, the rebellion in the West in 1549 and Dudley's attempt to put Lady Jane Grey on the throne, but he revives and interests us in all those remote theological debates, for he is himself caught up in them. He moves so easily in the past that his sober, formal style takes its distinctive flavour from his source documents. This chapter ending from volume one may illustrate some characteristics of his style:

Three months after this, at the age of fourscore years and more, died William Warham. A man of virtue, ability, and eloquence, he had been at the head of the Church almost from the beginning of this troubled century. The last public act in which he was engaged, the Submission of the Clergy, broke his heart: and before he died, he committed to writing a solemn protestation against any statutes hitherto published, or there-

107

after to be made by Parliament, in derogation of the Roman Pontiff and the Apostolic See, or in diminution of the ecclesiastical power, or of the rights, privileges, customs and liberties which belonged to the prerogative of his Church of Canterbury. 'We', he said, 'Archbishop of Canterbury, Primate of All England, and Legate of the Apostolic See, protest publicly and expressly, for ourselves and our metropolitical Church of Canterbury, that we cannot consent to such statutes: we dissent from them, cry out against them, contradict them.' But this weak exprobation itself was the last instrument of an English primate who died legate of the Apostolic See: and when the hand that wrote it, stiff in death, but wearing still in funeral state the consecrated glove in which it had oft been raised to celebrate the great mystery of the Catholic faith, was pressing to the yet unburied breast of the writer the golden cross of Canterbury, the proud dominion of a thousand years was already gone for ever. The scene was clearing for the new actors. The king had already been some time possessed of his new minister and counsellor in chief. He now got, within a few months of one another, his new Lord Keeper, his new Archbishop, his new wife, his new father-in-law, and all that belonged to them. (i. 143–4.)

Straightway, from the inversion in the first sentence we are aware that a conscious stylist is at work, violating the customary word order in the interests of rhythm. In the first three-quarters of the paragraph polysyllabic words of Latin origin, used seemingly for the sake of rhythmical elaboration, are numerous enough—and in the cases of 'exprobation' and 'metropolitical' unfamiliar enough—to be noticeable. One nineteenth-century reviewer, indeed, complained of Dixon's 'barbarous Latinized words'. The sentence structure is less latinized, but the climax of this paragraph, the sentence beginning 'But this weak exprobation', has something in it of the Ciceronian period, suspended by parentheses and at once copious and elegant. Here the mere statement of an historical fact is pleasingly heightened both by the feeling for verbal rhythm and by the visual imagination of the poet. This complex sentence is followed by the deliberate anticlimax of two simple sentences and an emphatic use of the colloquial 'got' as Dixon,

launching forward in his story, descends rapidly from Warham's deathbed to the domestic arrangements of Henry
VIII. In the last sentence of all we may detect a faint irony
just below the surface of the narrative.

Such an unobtrusive, dry humour continually enlivens
the *History*. There is a refined and charming sarcasm, for
instance, in this account of the last years of Dr. Layton,
Henry VIII's monastic visitor:

> The greatest of the Visitors, for so he must be considered in
> respect both of the length and efficiency of his services, retired to
> the well earned promotion of the Deanery of York: where, if
> virtue be best rewarded by the prospect of her deeds, he reposed
> in view of the ruins of St. Mary's and St. Leonard's. (ii. 197.)

But the humour is only to be appreciated fully in its context
for it does not lend itself to quotation. This is true of all the
features of Dixon's prose. As in *Mano*, so in the *History*, the
style is in the architecture, not the ornamentation, and
there are no 'purple passages' that may be extracted and
anthologized. The writing has dignity and spaciousness,
elegance and strength and broad sweeping rhythms, but
stylistic devices are subordinated to the primary purpose of
arguing clearly and keeping the narrative moving forward
continuously.

The style, as always, is the man. The writer's personality,
his imagination, poet's craftsmanship, wit, learning and
charity, are stamped firmly upon these six lengthy but
eminently readable volumes which make up one of the most
important of those many works of scholarship that were
written in nineteenth-century vicarages.

The reputation of Dixon's *History* stood high at his death,
but his poetry was still little known. So Bridges made a
selection from the unpublished verse and had it published
under the title of *The Last Poems of R. W. Dixon*. To it
Mary Coleridge contributed an enthusiastic Preface. Un-
fortunately Bridges had had to make the best of the small
quantity of manuscript verse put into his hands, and with
some justification was dissatisfied with *Last Poems*. Only

two hymns, two sonnets and 'Low River', a description of
the River Coquet at Warkworth, correspond with the title
of the book or add much to Dixon's reputation. The other
poems had been written before 1882 and Dixon himself had
deliberately excluded them from his Daniel Press publications.

The most impressive of *Last Poems* are those which convey Dixon's mood after his dark depression of spirit in 1892.
These, the hymn 'O Lord my God' and the sonnets 'To
Hope' and 'To Peace', are full of his characteristic pure-
heartedness and meekness. The 'hymn' is a simple private
prayer expressing humility and hope:

> O Lord my God, when sore bested
>   My evil life I do bewail,
> What times the life I might have led
>   Arising smites me like a flail:
>
> When I regard the past of sin,
>   Till sorrow drown me like despair;
> The saint in me that might have been
>   With that I am when I compare:
>
> Then grant the life that might have been
>   To be in fact through penitence;
> All my past years discharged of sin,
>   And spent in grace and innocence:
>
> And grant that I, when I forecast,
>   And shrink in fear of coming things,
> May take this comfort of the past,
>   And lay it on my imaginings.

The sonnets are more weighty and subtle; they complement
one another and together recreate a profoundly felt religious
experience:

> Fair Hope, that once, fair Hope, my prisoned heart
>   Delightedst with thy lustre, piercing night
> With eyelet twinkle, now thy former part
>   Renew, with thy one beam my heart delight;

110

Starlike, not sunlike, not scattering the dark,
  Spreading in prisons, thee I ask to shine;
Only to pierce, not scatter, with thy spark
  As stars the night, such night wherein I pine.

Then move some space in heaven: but let thy beam
  Solace me still: and I shall know and feel
Thy cluster near, the sisters of thy team,
  Which in the night above our day do wheel:
Faith, love are there, where Hope on high doth glide,
  Though further, fainter, in heaven's depth they ride.

O Peace, O Dove, O shape of the Holy Ghost,
  I would not vex thee with too subtle thought,
Put thee in fear by hopes, send thee to coast
  Regions unknown for what I dearest sought.
To rough delights I would not open course,
  Nor thy composure fray with vague desire,
Nor aspiration hold that did thee force,
  Nor move a step that I could not retire.

Nay, nay, I pray thee, close thy startled eye,
  Compose again thy self-stirred plumes, nor aim
At other station, in timidity
  Of fancied plots, which here I all disclaim.
Well, fly then! for perchance from heavenward flight
  Gentler on me thou mayst again alight.

These evocations of Dixon's hard-won spiritual peace provide a complete contrast with his puzzled and highly obscure speculations upon the resurrection of the body in
'Dust and Wind', or with the incoherent cry of despair
found in 'The Unknown King', a poem which Dixon left
incomplete when he 'lost the clue'.

Four years after *Last Poems* was published Bridges made
a more determined effort to popularize Dixon when he
edited the admirable *Selected Poems . . . with a Memoir*. The
Memoir is a fine tribute of affection; it remains the best
account of Dixon, and might be claimed to be one of the
best appreciations by any English poet of another. The only

111

faults in the selection of poems are an over-exclusive devotion to lyrics and a deliberate omission of the 'most remarkable work', but these were inevitable in view of Bridges's limited space and the need to appeal to an unadventurous verse-reading public. The collection includes eight hitherto unpublished poems, of which all but one (the sonnet 'To Sleep') were certainly written by 1881. Three—the moving 'O Ubi? Nusquam' (see p. 116 below) and two songs, 'Fallen Rain' (see p. 118 below) and 'Ruffling Wind', that anthropomorphize Nature with Dixon's usual delicacy and almost remind us of Blake—rank with the best of his work.

Selected Poems was well reviewed, but did not attract many new readers to Dixon. The centenary of his birth passed unnoticed except for a short article in *The Bookman*, and stocks of the seventy-year-old editions of *Christ's Company* and *Historical Odes* were not sold out until after the publication in 1935 of Professor Abbott's *The Correspondence of G. M. Hopkins and R. W. Dixon*. Professor Abbott printed a new poem by Dixon, 'The Secret Execution'. No more new poems have come to light since then,[1] but it is possible that more verse awaits discovery, for it is unlikely that the manuscript of Dixon's poems which Daniel had in his hands and was considering printing in April 1903 has been destroyed, unless by accident, and the 'love-tale and several minor poems' that Bridges withheld from *Last Poems*[2] have yet to be found. We do not know whether these manuscripts handled by Mrs. Dixon, Bridges and Daniel after Dixon's death were copies made by Hopkins or Bridges (or even Dixon) of early poems that were subsequently destroyed in Dixon's mental depression of 1892, or early poems, possibly religious, that were not destroyed, or poems written after 1892. If the lost poems were written in the last eight years of Dixon's life—the years which produced 'To Peace'—then we may well be sorry that they are

---

[1] Among letters by Dixon in the Library of Worcester College, Oxford, is a hymn which I print in an Appendix on page 122, but I cannot claim that it is certainly Dixon's.

[2] See *Selected Poems*, pp. 194, 195.

lost. But if they are earlier, and are in fact poems referred to in letters by Hopkins and Bridges then it is likely that they would not add much to our understanding of Dixon, and so our loss is not so great. For the titles of these poems and the comments made upon them by Hopkins and Bridges suggest that they are not unlike the bulk of the published verse which is, in attitudes and language, the typical production of a minor Victorian romantic poet writing under the shadows of Keats, Coleridge and Wordsworth.

Dixon fell naturally into the romantic attitudes. His Methodist upbringing and experiences within the Brotherhood, influenced by Keats and Ruskin and the after effects of the Oxford Movement, had made him profoundly dissatisfied with what he took to be a complacent and unjust society motivated by shallow, intellectual philosophies. He hungered after a fuller spiritual life and, together with his meteorosophistical Oxford Brothers, went 'sighing after the infinite'. He felt that he was an exile in his own age, and so he made in his imagination the aesthetic withdrawal into that ideal, timeless and unchanging Gothick world that Keats, Fouqué and Coleridge had painted. Neo-medievalism, widespread in many forms over many groups of nineteenth-century artists took for Dixon the form of that second generation Pre-Raphaelitism adopted by the friends of his youth. He was drawn into the Pre-Raphaelite movement (if it may be said that those individualistic artists ever made up a single 'movement') not primarily by his agreement with Holman Hunt's theories about art, but by the pietism which once had prompted him to join the Order of Sir Galahad, by his boyish love of Gothick tales of terror and of all things medieval, by Ruskin's teaching upon Christian art, and above all by the electric personality of Dante Gabriel Rossetti whose poetry and painting led him into a remote visionary world. So in the 'dream-born, dream-nursed' 'La Faerie' in 'Dream', in the 'Crosses of Love' narratives, which could be described as 'dreams, dreamed within another dream', and in other poems of that kind in *Christ's Company* and *Historical Odes* Dixon rejects life and

113

retires into a private other world. This earlier verse is filled with the stock properties and the attitudes of second generation Pre-Raphaelitism. We find deathly images, such as the dark, sinister pools in 'Despair' and 'The Wanderer', medieval costume, an archaic vocabulary, an enjoyment of the thrill of the macabre, a devotional feeling for sensuous beauty and a joy in decoration for its own sake. We hear, too, that low note of regret and resignation, sharpening at long intervals into a cry of despair, that will always be part of Dixon's characteristic tune.

However, Dixon's early Pre-Raphaelitism did not develop into the exclusive aestheticism of, for instance, the verse of Morris's middle period, and so the best of his maturer work (*Mano*, the later odes and a few songs) is more deeply satisfying than anything Morris wrote after *The Defence of Guenevere*. This is not unduly to belittle Morris who harmonized his poetic means and ends much better than Dixon and on comparison of total achievement must be reckoned the better poet. From the beginning Dixon felt that poetry was something more serious and deeply engaging than a merely decorative art like tapestry weaving. So he stiffened his early pictorial verse, the kind of verse that was 'easy to write', with what Professor Bush calls 'a lumpy backbone' of philosophizing, and contrived a kind of Christianized Keatsian verse that was often laboured and flat. He wrote more easily when he tried to make serious verse not out of public themes but out of his own direct private experience, especially his experiences of loneliness, old age, melancholy and that very conflict of claims which arose from his impulse to retire back into the aesthetic dream world. His attempts to write a more inclusive and serious poetry were not consistent or wholehearted, for the pull of the exclusive fantasy world of aesthetic withdrawal was strong, and particularly strong upon a poet who had virtually no audience. It is not surprising that his successes are few.

Dixon's poetry of experience is characterized by an unease and sadness that stem variously from his mental

conflict between the claims of art and of social and religious
duty, from his sense that he had lost a precious vision, and
from those religious doubtings that it was difficult for thinking men to avoid in the later nineteenth century. The lost
vision which he mourned was partly that shadowy land of
lost content of romantic myth but it was, too, his memory
of the Brotherhood days. In the intense idealism of those
Oxford years he had had some intuition of the mystical
unity and harmony of all life—which he proclaims in 'St.
Paul', 'St. John', 'Rapture' and 'Orpheus'—and had felt
a sense of joyful purposefulness in his own life. But this
awareness of unity and this personal joy were lost, and
'Inscience' (p. 49 above) and 'Ode on Departing Youth'
record the sobering moment of disenchantment, 'the check,
the change, the fall', when youth's visions fade. 'To Summer' (pp. 45, 46 above) ends in a spiritual winter of disil-
lusionment and much of the verse in *Historical Odes* and the
later volumes is full of an autumnal imagery that reflects
Dixon's feeling of deprivation. His most considered comment on the human situation, *Mano*, shows bewildered man
tossed by the caprice of Fate in a disintegrating and decaying world, and leaves us in no doubt that the vision of joy
and purpose has faded. Disenchantment, loneliness and
mutability are the recurrent themes of Dixon's maturer
verse. But in 'The Unknown King' and in a number of
poems upon the impersonal vastness and vacancy of the
universe there are expressions of dark pessimism that suggest a pathological melancholy perhaps comparable with
Dixon's condition in his illness of 1891–2:

Here I wander about, and here I mournfully ponder:
Weary to me is the sun, weary the coming of night:
Here is captivity still, there would be captivity yonder:
Like to myself are the rest, smitten is all with a blight . . .

Where is the pitying grace, that once was prayer's incentive,
Where is the ear that heard, and the face that once answered to
    face?

                    ('The Silent Heavens' in *Last Poems*)

It is clear that at some period after his optimistic youth
Dixon found himself in the same predicament as many of
his contemporaries, 'wandering between two worlds', unable to find full comfort in faith and recoiling from scepti-
cism. Indeed, he did not fully adjust his personal hopes and
fears until he wrote the hymns and the sonnets 'To Peace'
and 'To Hope' (p. 110 above) in the last decade of his life.

Like other romantic poets Dixon writes about himself by
writing about external nature. He projects his own states of
feeling into the scenes he describes and thus knows himself
in his vision of them. So in 'O Ubi? Nusquam' the 'solemn
pain' is the poet's and the occasion of the emotion is stated:

> She comes not: in the summer night
> The trembling river runneth bright.
> O look again, fond heart of love,
> On darkling earth, on heaven above.
>
> Behold, the poplar trees divide
> The long-drawn space where sunset died:
> There still is the redly ebbing light
> Dying beneath the hand of night.
>
> The cloud-bars now with solemn pain
> Upclose, and all is wrapped in rain:
> Ah no, that sky holds not her form;
> It is the altar of the storm.
>
> Earth, that so many flowers hast,
> So many fields, such meadows vast,
> So many paths for gentle feet,
> Hast thou no place for her, most sweet?
>
> No, no: night's wimple creeps apace
> Upon thy coldly darkling face;
> Thy wind-swept trees bow low to me,
> Waving their hands in mockery.

Here, as in 'To Summer' and 'Ode on Advancing Age',
Dixon accepts the projective view of Nature; and it is
arguable, of course, that whenever he attributes emotional

116

activity to objects he must in fact be projecting his own feelings. But Dixon himself seems to claim from time to time that natural objects have some kind of emotional life of their own. That is, he takes the realist view of Nature, that behind the face of things is a metaphysical reality. In 'Rapture', whence he identifies the life inherent in Nature with immanent God, he abstracts from and reflects upon his vision, stating clearly the steps in the transition from his ordinary perception of the appearances of things to his extraordinary insight into the reality that lies behind these appearances. In those later poems where he sees into 'the life of things' he is less reflective and analytic and less obviously self-conscious. He seems to withdraw his own person as observer, to leave us only the informed, the living object as he 'dramatizes' natural phenomena in 'Sky that rollest ever' (p. 86 above), in 'Death and Victory', a strange but haunting piece of animism:

> He wept, he wept: there came a wind
> Out of the cloud heavy and blind:
> The angel of human thoughts had joy—
> And water dropped from the cloud's hair,
> The sun shone on the green leaves fair,
> The wood-side sparkled everywhere.
>
> He moaned: great pain weighed down his eyes;
> His knees were bent, thick came his sighs:
> The angel of human wounds had joy—
> The sad earth was bemired with rain,
> The ditches rose and stormed the plain,
> The eddying wind blew round again.
>
> He died: his head to earth was bowed,
> Then sudden lifted to the cloud:
> The angel of broken wings had joy—
> The sun grew strong in the thick air,
> The rainbow fled; half heaven was bare,
> The storm went off with wings aflare.
> (*Selected Poems*, p. 152),

and in that other, more generally admired, rainbow piece,
'Fallen Rain':

> Silent fell the rain
> To the earthly ground;
> Then arose a sound
>   To complain:
>
> Why am I cast down
> From the cloud so sweet,
> Trampled by the feet
>   Of the clown?
>
> Why was I drawn through
> All the Rainbow bright,
> Who her smile did light
>   Me to woo?
>
> Then my tremblings ceased;
> To the smile I bowed,
> And the weeping cloud
>   Me released:—
>
> Then the cruel smile
> Flashed like agony,
> And I fall and die
>   Through a wile.

Both poems display a very different word painting technique from that employed in 'Rapture'. There Dixon had
attempted to depict the forms of Nature with the close
attention to surface detail of a Tennyson or a Holman Hunt.
Here he has turned to an impressionist technique by which
he attempts to capture the immediate and momentary
'temper' of light, shade, form and movement in a scene,
and at his best communicates, as Hopkins said, 'a delightful
freshness of out-of-doors.' Both poems display, too, the
delicacy and delightful freshness of Dixon's imagination,
but 'Death and Victory' is the less successful as a coherent
poetic statement because its elements—an experience of the
shifting, vaporous brilliance of the contention of wind, rain

and sun in a summer rainstorm, the familiar Dixonian concept of a 'sad earth' and the enigmatic angels and sacrificial victim who appear to have drifted in out of Dixon's Pre-Raphaelite phase—are not fused.

Despite 'Death and Victory' it is broadly true that Dixon's verse ran clearer towards the end. Early in life he probably wrote hastily and without sufficient revision. The Pre-Raphaelite group was a bad school for apprentice poets, and the same kind of amateurish impatience and failure to master techniques that ruined the Oxford Union murals marred a great deal of Dixon's verse in *Christ's Company* and *Historical Odes*. Later he had a surer control of his craft and could benefit, too, from the advice of Hopkins and Bridges, but his verse writing was restricted by work on the *History*, by sickness (for he found that composition was 'an excitement that can only be borne by health') and, in the last years, by his renunciation of secular verse. He did not apply himself to the craft of poetry as Bridges and Hopkins did. Except in a handful of songs and odes and *Mano* he did not find his own idiom. His failures are many and the field of his successes is small. Judged by his bad poetry only he appears as an incompetent versifier who copied Keats and Coleridge in his youth and Wordsworth and Coleridge in his manhood. But in his good work there is ample evidence of integrity and true imagination, even when there is a partial failure to get an experience quite into focus, to communicate fully and to interpret. He masters poetically only a small area of experience, for in the shorter poems nearly all his best work is in a thin imaginative vein where he uses certain autumnal scenes to express a personal awareness of mortality. Working within a narrow range of subjects and moods he employed what Hopkins called 'astonishingly clear an inward eye to see what is in visible nature' and 'a deep insight into what is earnest, tender and pathetic in human life and feeling' to produce a few short poems that rank with the best in the language. *Mano*, further, has the proportion, discipline and depth of an important work of art, and on it Dixon stakes his claim for serious attention as a poet. We have an uneasy feeling that this neglected poem is not the work of a negligible writer. The reputation of the *History* as a work of scholarship and art is, of course, fairly widely acknowledged and is secure.

In middle age, in the face of indifference, loneliness and the pressure of other work, Dixon kept to 'the spirit and grandeur of poetry' and, until his critical illness, practised his art with the pure-hearted and serious devotion appropriate to it. In his verse Hopkins found 'an extreme purity, a directness of human nature, and absence of affectation which is most rare', and added, 'I feel in reading him what a gentleman he is and it brings on the feeling that I am a blackguard.' Everything in his life from the idealism of the Order of Sir Galahad to the loving kindness of his Warkworth ministry ran counter to the general spiritual vulgarity of his age. The same candour, modesty, delicacy, gentleness and sympathy fill his life, his verse, his *History* and his letters. (The letters which comforted and encouraged Hopkins in his dry time must be reckoned as Dixon's very important indirect contribution to English poetry.) His life and writings alike harmoniously expressed his diligence, devotion, humility, humour and comprehensive charity. He was a virtuous man without personal ambition who loved God, Nature and man. He won respect from men, and from one of those who knew him well earned the magnanimous and affectionate tribute which most fittingly may stand as his memorial and conclude this study:

Some characters give the idea of a personality that has attained to certain qualities; in others we seem to see qualities composing a character. . . . Dixon was of the latter type. His imagination, since that is an inborn gift beyond conscious control, would, of course, have this effect, and seem a visitation from without, and he merely the happy dispenser of it. His insight, clear judgment, and memory were gifts of a similar kind; but even in his humility he did not appear like a man who had put it on, but as an incarnation of the quality, whose essence was distilled or reflected in him. And so with his good temper, humour, patience, tenderness, and sympathy, which made up his social aspect, all seemed to flow from the deeper perennial sources, uncontaminated and inexhaustible. This great ingenuous being went about among men almost unrecognised, though influencing nearly everyone with whom he came in contact. As he respected every man, he won respect from all, and any lengthened intercourse with him awoke the best affinities of his associates, who became infected with his grace. One might see around him the common Christian virtues propagating themselves in a natural state like healthy plants that, without a gardener's care, flourish and multiply from year to year. He was truly revered, and where he bestowed his affection the gift was so unmeasured that the mere flattery of it must have been injurious, were it not that spiritual love has no excess, but is always beneficent. It was more than any one could repay, and, however I have rejoiced in it, the remembrance, now that he is taken away, shames me with the thought of my unworthiness.[1]

[1] *Selected Poems*, pp. xlv, xlvi.

APPENDIX

A Poem among Dixon's Letters in Worcester College Library

This poem, undated, is among Dixon's letters to Daniel; it is written in a hand that is not Dixon's, but could be Mrs. Dixon's.

This is the time when I must pray,
  Because to pray I know not how,
For I am near Despair today;
  My only hope, O Lord, art Thou.

This is the day which Thou didst know
  Was coming on me, when Thy love
Cheered and refreshed me long ago,
  And gave a glimpse of joys above.

This is the hour when most I need
  To see Thee hanging on the tree,
And feel that Thou in very deed
  Didst give Thy precious blood for me.

This is the day and this the hour,
  This moment have I need of Thee—
Now, when I feel the bad dark power
  That seems almost too strong for me.

For while I call it dark and bad,
  And use the words that Thou hast given
I all but feel I should be glad
  To think there were no hell or heaven.

I *all but* feel it: yet I cry
  Out of the very darkest deep,
And know that I am heard on high,
  And that Thy love my soul doth keep.

I cannot see Thee as Thou art,
  I cannot feel, what feel I would,
I cannot now lift up my heart,
  And yet I know that Thou art good.

Good and most merciful art Thou;
  O King of pity give me tears,
Silent before Thee let me bow,
  And tell Thee all my griefs and fears.

A broken and a contrite heart
  I know Thou wilt not Lord despise:
Broken and crushed I am, Thou art
  My King, my Lord, my Sacrifice.

O teach me, teach me how to pray;
  Break my hard heart and loose my tongue:
And lo for me in heaven today
  Shall songs of praise, dear Lord, be sung.

BIBLIOGRAPHY

I. The Published Writings of R. W. Dixon

VERSE

(This list omits selections containing no new work by Dixon.)

The Sicilian Vespers, a Prize Poem, Birmingham, 1852.

Christ's Company and Other Poems, London, 1861.

S. John in Patmos, the Prize Poem on a Sacred Subject for 1863, Oxford and London, 1863.

Historical Odes and Other Poems, London, 1864.

'Perished Ideals' in *Sonnets of Three Centuries*, edited by T. Hall Caine, London, 1882.

Mano, a Poetical History, London, 1883.

Odes and Eclogues, Daniel Press, Oxford, 1884.

Lyrical Poems, Daniel Press, Oxford, 1887.

The Story of Eudocia and her Brothers, Daniel Press, Oxford, 1888.

Mano, a Poetical History ('Second Edition'),[1] London, 1891.

---

[1] Correctly a second impression. The title page of some copies of the 1883 edition in the original blue cloth binding was cancelled and a cancel title carrying the words 'Second Edition' and the date 1891 was pasted on to the stub of its conjugate leaf. C4 was similarly cancelled in order to make verbal alterations on C4^v (p. 24). Finally, an advertisement leaf carrying 'Opinions on the First Edition' was pasted between the half-title and endpaper. I know of only three copies in this state, one of which is in the Bodleian.

The first and only edition of *Mano* was of five hundred copies published by Routledge at the author's cost in 1883. One hundred and thirty copies were sold in the first year, but sales were very slow thereafter. In 1891, it seems, someone suggested and paid for the 'second edition' described above. Certainly Dixon wrote to him on 31 August, 'Your generosity to your contemporaries is one of the warm places not only in contemporary but in all literary history. . . . I shall proceed with the edition of Mano as quickly as I can'. In the letter Dixon enclosed his manuscript sheet of 'Opinions on the First Edition' for the printer. However, any hope that the unknown benefactor or Dixon may have had of pushing sales by the questionable device of a spurious second edition was unfulfilled. In July 1895 Dixon told Bridges that sales had 'ceased entirely' and that he had decided to give away the remaining bound copies. I do not know whether he alluded to the 1883 or the 1891 impression or both. The publisher's remaindered unbound sheets were bought by the Oxford University Press after Dixon's death and

In Obitum Edwini Hatch, D.D., Carmen Elegiacum, London, 1892.

Songs and Odes, London, 1896 (Elkin Mathew's *Shilling Garland* No. 5.).

The Last Poems of Richard Watson Dixon, D.D., selected and edited by Robert Bridges, with a Preface by M. E. Coleridge, London, 1905.

Poems by the late Rev. Dr. Richard Watson Dixon, a Selection with Portrait and a Memoir by Robert Bridges, London, 1909.

'The Secret Execution' in *The Correspondence of Gerard Manley Hopkins and Richard Watson Dixon*, edited by Claude Colleer Abbott, London, 1935.

PROSE

(a) *Separate publications*

The Close of the Tenth Century of the Christian Era, the Arnold Prize Essay for 1858, Oxford, 1858.

The Life of James Dixon, D.D., Wesleyan Minister, London, 1874.

An Essay on the Maintenance of the Church of England as an Established Church, London, 1874.

History of the Church of England from the Abolition of the Roman Jurisdiction, London:

Vol. I, 1878; second ed. revised 1884; third ed. revised 1895.
Vol. II, 1881; second ed. revised 1887; third ed. revised 1895.
Vol. III, 1885; second ed. revised 1893.
Vol. IV, 1891.
Vols. V and VI, 1902.

A Sermon preached on the occasion of the Diamond Jubilee, Alnwick, 1897.[1]

The Correspondence of Gerard Manley Hopkins and Richard Watson Dixon, edited with notes and an Introduction by Claude Colleer Abbott, London, 1935; second (revised) impression, 1955.

issued, without the cancels, in a plain maroon cloth binding with a label on the spine. Stocks were exhausted in 1945 or 1947.

[1] I have been unable to trace any copy of this work, which is mentioned in Dixon's *Last Poems*, and in *D.N.B.*

(b) *Articles and Reviews*

The Oxford and Cambridge Magazine, London, 1856:
January, 'The Rivals'; February, 'The Barrier Kingdoms';
March, 'The Prospects of Peace'. (All unsigned.)

The London Quarterly Review, London:
January 1857, 'Gothic Art and John Ruskin'.
October 1860, 'Modern Painters, Volume Five'.
(Both unsigned; the first is not certainly by Dixon, but see
Correspondence, p. 52, footnote.)

*Transactions of the Cumberland and Westmoreland Antiquarian
and Archaeological Society*, IV. 1879:
'The Monastic Comperta, so far as they regard the Religious
Houses of Cumberland and Westmorland'.

The Dictionary of National Biography, London:

Vol. VI,	1886, 'Samuel Bradburn, 1751–1816'.
Vol. VII,	1886, 'George Browne, D.D., d. 1556'.
	'Agnes Bulmer, 1775–1836'.
Vol. IX,	1887, 'John Cardmaker, d. 1555'.
Vol. XII,	1887, 'Sir Robert Constable, 1478?–1537'.
	'Richard Cox, 1500–1581'.
Vol. XIV,	1888, 'George Day, 1501?–1556'.
Vol. XV,	1888, 'James Dixon, 1788–1871'.
	'John Dobson, 1787–1865'.
Vol. XVI	1888, 'John Dudley, 1502?–1553'.
Vol. XXIII,	1890, 'James Haddon, fl. 1556'.
Vol. XXIV,	1890, 'John Hales, d. 1571'.

(All signed. The article on Lord Guildford Dudley, vol. XVI,
1888, is 'from notes supplies by the Rev. Canon R. W.
Dixon'.)

The English Historical Review, London:
July 1886, *Troubles connected with the Prayer Book of 1549.
Documents* ... edited by N. Pocock.
October 1889, *Life of Blessed John Fisher*, by T. E. Bridgett.
July 1891, *Edward VI and the Book of Common Prayer*, by
F. A. Gasquet and E. Bishop.
October 1891, *Acts of the Privy Council, New Series, Vols. I
and II*, edited by J. R. Dasent.
April 1893, *Acts of the Privy Council, New Series, Vols. III
and IV*, edited by J. R. Dasent.

January 1894, *Acts of the Privy Council, New Series, Vols. V and VI*, edited by J. R. Dasent.

July 1894, *Acts of the Privy Council, New Series, Vol. VII*, edited by J. R. Dasent.

January 1897, *Acts of the Privy Council, New Series, Vols. VIII to XII*, edited by J. R. Dasent.

October 1897, *The Last Abbott of Glastonbury and his Companions*, by F. A. Gasquet.

July 1899, *Letters and Papers of the reign of Henry VIII*, arranged and catalogued by James Gairdner and B. H. Brodie.

(All signed reviews.)

VERSE AND PROSE EDITED BY DIXON

The Bible Birthday Book, arranged by the Rev. Canon Dixon, London, 1887.

Seven Sermons, preached in the Cathedral Church of Newcastle on Tyne, November 1887, London 1888. (With a Preface by Dixon.)

II. SOURCE MATERIALS

UNPUBLISHED MANUSCRIPTS

(a) *In private hands*

'The Life of Edwin Hatch' by his widow.

Correspondence of Dixon and Robert Bridges, 1880–1899.

Letters from Dixon to Edwin Hatch, 1857, 1866 and 1873; to D. G. Rossetti, 1875; to Henry Daniel, 1886–1895; to Edmund Routledge, 1886; to Mrs. M. Bridges, 1889–1891; to A. H. Miles, 1892; to Edmund Gosse, 1894; to Miss Hatch, 1896–1897; and to Henry Newbolt, 1896.

Letters to Dixon from D. G. Rossetti, 1875; from A. C. Swinburne, 1883; and from Sir Edward Burne-Jones, 1897.

Letters to Henry Daniel from Robert Bridges, 1880–1895; and from Mary Coleridge, 1896.

A letter from John Ruskin to Thomas McNicholl, 1861.

(b) *In public collections*

In the Bodleian Library:

MS.,Don.e.20, which consists mainly of letters written between March and May 1900 to the Rev. Wilkin Rees from forty-five correspondents, most of whom knew Dixon personally. It includes letters from Dixon to Cormell Price, 1873 (fol. 88), and Thomas Bushby, 1899 (fol. 29), and extracts of letters from Dixon to Mackenzie Bell, 1884–1899 (fol. 7–10). Rees was collecting material for a magazine article on Dixon which, as far as I know, was never written.

MS.,Eng.Lett.d.143: Letters from Robert Bridges to Mrs. C. Hopkins and Miss K. Hopkins.

In the British Museum:

Add.MS.44,520,fol.165–167: Letters from Dixon to Rev. S. E. Gladstone and to Rt. Hon. W. E. Gladstone, 1895.

In the Library of Worcester College, Oxford:

Letters from Dixon to Robert Bridges, 1883; to Henry Daniel, 1884–1895; and to Sir Thomas Herbert Warren, 1898.

A letter from Mrs. M. Dixon to Henry Daniel, 1903.

In the William Morris Gallery, Walthamstow:

Letters from Dixon to J. M. Mackail, 1899.

Dixon's reminiscences of his Oxford years, written for Mackail.

Notebooks and papers of Mackail containing material he collected for use in writing his *Life of William Morris.*

PUBLISHED WORKS

C. C. Abbott (ed.), *Correspondence of Gerard Manley Hopkins and Richard Watson Dixon*, revised, 1955.

C. C. Abbott (ed.), *Letters of Gerard Manley Hopkins to Robert Bridges*, revised, 1955.

C. C. Abbott (ed.), *Further Letters of Gerard Manley Hopkins*, second ed., revised and enlarged, 1956.

H. C. Beeching, 'R. W. Dixon' in *Supplement to the Dictionary of National Biography*, 1901.

Robert Bridges, 'Memoir' in *Poems by the late Rev. Richard Watson Dixon*, 1909. (Reprinted in *Three Friends*, 1932.)

H. J. Bulkeley, *In Memory of Canon Dixon*, a Sermon preached in Warkworth Church on the Sunday morning after he died, 1900.

G. Burne-Jones, *Memorials of Edward Burne-Jones*, two vols., 1904.

Mary Coleridge, 'The Last Hermit of Warkworth' in *Non Sequitur*, 1900.

Louise Creighton, *Life and Letters of Mandell Creighton*, two vols., 1904.

Lucy Crump (ed.), *Letters of George Birbeck Hill*, 1906.

R. W. Dixon, *The Life of James Dixon, D.D., Wesleyan Minister*, 1874.

Henry Gee, Preface to volume v of R. W. Dixon's *History of the Church of England*, 1902.

E. Gosse, *Life of Algernon Charles Swinburne*, 1917.

T. Hall Caine, *Recollections of Dante Gabriel Rossetti*, 1882.

G. B. Hill, *Writers and Readers*, 1892.

G. B. Hill (ed.), *Letters of Dante Gabriel Rossetti to William Allingham, 1854–1870*, 1897.

W. H. Hutton (ed.), *Robert Gregory, 1819–1911, the Autobiography*, 1912.

G. Lafourcade, *Swinburne, a Literary Biography*, 1932.

J. W. Mackail, *Life of William Morris*, new ed., two vols., 1901.

J. W. Mackail, *William Morris and his Circle*, 1907.

Douglas Macleane, *A History of Pembroke College, Oxford*, (Publications of the Oxford Historical Society, vol. 33), 1897.

Falconer Madan, 'Bibliography of the Daniel Press' in *The Daniel Press, Memorials of C. H. O. Daniel with a Bibliography of the Press, 1845–1919*, 1921.

A. H. Miles, 'Richard Watson Dixon' in *Poets and Poetry of the Century*, vol. v, *Charles Kingsley to James Thomson*, 1893.

Henry Newbolt, *My World as in my Time*, 1932.

S. Nowell-Smith, 'Bridges, Hopkins and Dr. Daniel' in *Times Literary Supplement*, 13 December 1957, p. 764.

S. Nowell-Smith, 'Some Uncollected Authors XXIX—Richard Watson Dixon' in *The Book Collector*, Autumn 1961, p. 322.

Oxford and Cambridge Magazine, 1856.

W. Rothenstein, *Men and Memories, Recollections*, vol. i, 1931.

The Times, 25 January 1900, p. 6, obituary notice of R. W. Dixon.

INDEX

131